THE ADVENTURES
OF
DR. ALPHABET

The Adventures of Dr. Alphabet

104 Unusual Ways to Write Poetry in the Classroom and the Community

by Dave Morice

Teachers & Writers Collaborative

New York

The Adventures of Dr. Alphabet

Teachers & Writers Collaborative
5 Union Square West
New York, New York 10003–3306

JPT
372.64
MOR

Library of Congress Cataloguing-in-Publication Data
Morice, Dave, 1946–
    The adventures of Dr. Alphabet : 101 unusual ways to write poetry in the classroom and the community
    / by Dave Morice
        p.   cm.
    Includes bibliography.
    ISBN 0-915924-44-7
    1. Poetry--Study and teaching (Elementary) 2. Poetry--Study and teaching. 3. Poetry--Authorship--Study and teaching (Elementary) 4. Poetry--Authorship--Study and teaching.   I. Title. II. Title: Adventures of Doctor Alphabet.
LB1575.M67   1995
372.64044--dc20   94-38914
                                                    CIP

Cover photo: Dom Franco
Illustrations: Dave Morice
Design: Chris Edgar
Printed by Philmark Lithographics, N.Y.

Acknowledgments

Special thanks to the following people. To Paula Brandt, Carol Vogt, Donilee Popham, and Mary Ellen Alberhansky at the University of Iowa Curriculum Lab for so much help in locating books. To Bob McCown in the University of Iowa Library Special Collections Department for giving me instant access to the archives. To Dennett Hutchcroft for the idea for the Mr. and Ms. Poetryhead exercise. To Dom Franco for the cover photograph and some of the photographs in the text. To the teachers and administrators who invited me into their schools, and to the students of all ages who turned their enthusiasm and creativity into poetry.

A tip of the Alphabet Hat to Ron Padgett and Chris Edgar for their invaluable suggestions and encouraging comments, and to Ron for the title of this book.

•

Teachers & Writers Collaborative receives funds from the New York State Council on the Arts, the National Endowment for the Arts, and the New York City Department of Cultural Affairs.

Teachers & Writers Collaborative's programs and publications are also supported by contributions from the American Stock Exchange, Bertelsmann USA, The Bingham Trust, the Bydale Foundation, Chemical Bank, Consolidated Edison, the Aaron Diamond Foundation, NYNEX Corporation, New York Times Company Foundation, Henry Nias Foundation, Helena Rubinstein Foundation, the Scherman Foundation, and the Lila Wallace-Reader's Digest Fund.

For Jerry Watson

TABLE OF CONTENTS

Chapter 3. Environmental Poetry

Chapter 4. Wordplay Poetry

Poetry can do a hundred and one things, delight, sadden, disturb, amuse, instruct—it may express every possible shade of emotion, and describe every conceivable kind of event, but there is only one thing that all poetry must do; it must praise all it can for being and for happening.

—W. H. Auden, "Making, Knowing and Judging"

INTRODUCTION

He who wants to understand the poem
Must go to the land of poetry.

—Goethe, "West-östlicher Diwan"

EVER since Kenneth Koch's *Wishes, Lies, and Dreams* opened the door nationwide to using new poetry writing techniques in the classroom, many other teachers have invented their own methods. Some of these methods explore the principle of assigned topics and forms to engage students' imaginations.

The methods in this book are based on a different principle—that changing the physical elements of writing provides new ways to make poetry. Using these methods, students write in ways they have probably never tried before. They experiment with unfamiliar writing tools, writing surfaces, and writing environments. They try paint, whitewash, rubber stamps, cut-out words. They write on lamps, popsicle sticks, peanuts, and paper wrapped around school buildings. They use word lists, poker cards, and kaleidoscopes. And they write in the gym, on the playground, and even downtown.

This book has two purposes: to show more than a hundred ways to create poetry and to serve as a source of ideas for teachers. In the first case, the methods can be used as directed. In the second case, the teacher can take off from the basic concepts in order to design new methods.

In general, the methods here give directions for students to write and, in many cases, to do other things. Consequently, the term *activity* refers to *what* the students do, and *method* refers to *how* it is done. Put another way, each method describes an activity.

The teacher can use these activities with the students as frequently or infrequently as desired. For a well-rounded experience, the teacher should present them as alternatives to the usual ways people write.

Most of these methods have been tested in the classroom or a writing workshop. The students ranged in age from five to ninety-four. They enthusiastically tackled the challenges involved and wrote a lot of high-energy poetry. Many students and teachers have told me how much fun they had doing these activities; if there is one principle behind these methods, it is that if poetry writing is a pleasure, the students will want to write it.

About the Methods

All creative writing methods have one thing in common: they alter the writing process. In some cases, the alteration is slight—for instance, assigning a topic for a poem. Normally, people don't write poetry based on topics that other people give them.

Most students are used to the routine of writing with pencil and paper. However, replace the pencil and paper with fabric marker and a mirror, and suddenly new and intriguing challenges arise. The new writing tools and the shiny surface alter the routine. Now the physical act of writing becomes fresh in itself, for students of all ages.

Furthermore, because the results are open to personal interpretation, the students don't know exactly what their poems should say. This places the students in a position of equality, from which they define their own literary values. The methods in this book offer an enjoyable challenge that students can accomplish on their own terms.

Poetry Activities

These activities work in several ways. Many, like the Technicolor Page and the Poetry Castle, use paper in new ways. Others, like the Poetry Lamp and Hand Fan Writing, incorporate unusual writing tools and surfaces. Some, like the Spider Web of Words, take place in a special environment. Others are based on games, puzzles, and wordplay.

Most of the activities require some preparation. It's usually easy, such as photocopying material from this book. In a few cases, the preparation involves more work—cutting cards out, making small wooden sculptures, wrapping a piece of paper around the school. Students can help (and often want to help) with the preparation.

For several methods, common objects are necessary. They're inexpensive and easy to find. For two or three methods, you might have a harder time locating the exact same materials, but you can usually come up with a good substitute.

Student Poems

While most of the activities result in poems on paper, many of them generate poetry objects—lamps, mirrors, and other things with poetry written on them. Like art objects, they can be displayed in the classroom, the media center, and the public library. I've exhibited student work in all those places; photos of some of the displays appear here. The students' poems that come out of these activities tend to be imaginative and energetic. Depending on the method, the works may be realistic, surrealistic, lyrical, narrative, serious, or funny. The students delve into the activities with a sense of adventure and exploration.

Examples of student poems accompany most of the methods presented here. In some cases, the student poems retain their original spelling, punctuation, and capitalization. Most have no titles.

What Is Poetry?

I take a wide-angle view of poetry. To define it seems to require drawing a line in the literary sand to separate that which is from that which isn't. Because language is so malleable, closing off certain areas seems somewhat wasteful.

Still, words have definitions, and poetry is a word. My best definition: poetry is language organized, produced, and experienced as an art form. If someone believes something is poetry, then, as far as I'm concerned, it is poetry.

My main question becomes, "Is it good or bad poetry?" Here definitions don't work. Poetry follows Heisenberg's Uncertainty Principle. No matter what I hear about a poem, I can't know whether I like it until I read it. The very act of reading changes it.

The best poems affect the way I think about the world and about language. Their lines flash like lightning whose memory never goes away. They may shock by speaking the unspeakable, as in Shelley's "How beautiful is Death, / Death and his brother Sleep, / . . . And yet, so passing beautiful." Or tease by their simplicity, as in William Carlos Williams's "so much / depends / upon a red / wheel barrow." Or capture a feeling with intense clarity, as in Emily Dickinson's "I'm nobody! Who are you? / Are you—Nobody—too?" Or just plain entertain with their wit, as in E. E. Cummings's "may i feel said he / (i'll squeal said she."

Many contemporary writers are creating powerful verse in a multitude of forms. It's often as interesting to see the forms of their poetry as it is to read the content. They write free verse, prose poetry, concrete poetry, performance poetry, and even rhymed verse.

At the other extreme, my son, age six, has said things that have the feel of poetry. When he wants to talk about something, he doesn't always have the necessary vocabulary or grammar, so he improvises. His lack of language is both a disadvantage and an advantage. It keeps him from talking as an adult, yet it liberates him from the conventions of adult language. "I saw the bug go over to that glass kind of walkly." As he gets older, the wide-eyed language of childhood will fade away.

Through poetry, I can return to that wonderful time of life when language is continual discovery. I lost that feeling in grade school, but I regained it when I was in my twenties. After writing carefully structured poems for a couple of years, I decided to let it all go and type

3

whatever I wanted. For the first time since I was a child, I explored language anew.

After that personal discovery, I spent a lot of time writing. For a few years I thought of poetry as "a way of life," but such a view seemed to impose an artificial hierarchy on my interests—teaching and drawing had become just as important to me. I tried to think of poetry as "a way of looking at life," but that was too limiting. "A way of interpreting life" seemed too purposeful, "a way of being creative" too general.

Perhaps the poet Wallace Stevens defined it in the only possible way: "Poetry is poetry. . . ."

To Rhyme or Not to Rhyme

This question comes up often in schools. I tell the students that most poets don't rhyme, but some do. I let them know that I write both kinds of poetry, and that they can write whatever way they want.

Some students breathe a sigh of relief at hearing they don't have to rhyme. Others feel that a poem has to rhyme or it isn't poetry. Others enjoy the challenge of rhyming. Rhyme can be a useful tool in focusing attention on sound, word choice, and structure. For variety, some of the activities require rhyming, and others require not rhyming. When I taught an older people's poetry class, about half of them started out rhyming. Within two months, the rhymers were writing free verse most of the time. None of the non-rhymers ever converted to rhyme.

What to Tell the Students

If the students have had any previous experience with poetry, they probably realize that classroom writing methods differ from "real-world" techniques. Still, to make sure they're aware of some basic distinctions, I introduce the methods something like this: "People normally write poetry alone. They use pencils, pens, typewriters, or computers. They think in advance about what they're going to write, and they rewrite what they've written. But today we're going to do it a different way."

When I started teaching a Poetry Class for People over Sixty, in 1975, I assigned topics, such as "My Oldest Memory" or "My Personal Unsolved Mystery." The assigned topics worked fine, but after a couple of months, everyone became too familiar with each other's style. I thought it would be good to try other approaches, so I looked for ideas in articles and books. To my surprise, there wasn't a huge amount of information readily available on writing poetry in class. Kenneth Koch's *Wishes, Lies, and Dreams* was an exception. Koch's methods looked fresh and interesting, and his students' poems showed an amazing amount of creativity. I tried one of his methods with the older people,

4

and they enjoyed it. Spurred on by their enthusiastic response, I decided to make up some methods of my own. To do so, I looked to my writing experiences as Dr. Alphabet.

Actualism

In the early 1970s, Iowa City, where I live, was rampant with poetry of all kinds, ranging from the academic to the experimental. The poets divided themselves into two major camps: the Iowa Writers' Workshop (students in the M.F.A. program at the University of Iowa) and the non-Workshop "underground." Poets in the latter group banded together under the name of "Actualism," a term coined by the late Darrell Gray. I was an Actualist. A year earlier, I had been a Workshop student.

The Actualists brought poetry to the people. They wrote about common, everyday objects and experiences. They got together in their apartments to party and to write collaborative poems. They had readings at bookstores and bars. They held festivals in local church auditoriums.

The Iowa Writers Workshop seemed to confine poetry to the ivy tower of the English-Philosophy Building. In classes, students shared their poetry, but they didn't always enjoy it: they often attacked each other's poems with a vengeance. Poetry readings occurred on a weekly basis, but the poets appeared only in university classrooms or auditoriums, not in the community.

As an Actualist, I started writing poetry publicly at art festivals, bookstore openings, and other places. For festivals, I sometimes dressed as "Dr. Alphabet," in white shirt, pants, shoes, and top hat, all painted with colorful letters, and I carried an alphabet-spangled cane. I wrote

marathon poems—that is, poems written over a long period of time, space, or both. Poetry Marathon No. 1—1,000 poems in twelve hours— took place during the grand opening of Epstein's Book Store in Iowa City. It was exhausting and wonderful. I'd never had such a great time writing poetry. Some of the marathon poems required long, wide rolls of paper, and sometimes the writing tools varied in other ways: white-wash for painting giant words on a city street; a wide-tipped magic marker taped to the bottom of the Alphabet Cane for writing on paper taped around a city block; spray paint for writing a long line of words on a piece of paper taped along the pedestrian walkway crossing the Delaware River; and felt-tip pens for printing a poem on a dress worn by poet Joyce Holland on the "Tomorrow" show.

From Marathons to Methods

The marathon writing process seemed to operate under different laws of poetry. For the first time, I had dozens of collaborators. People I knew and people I didn't know looked over my shoulder and commented on the poem, suggested a word or phrase, and offered ideas. I wrote, but many other people contributed to the writing directly or indirectly. Sometimes they praised, and sometimes they criticized. I was at the wheel of a car full of backseat drivers, and I loved it!

The poems had something in common with contemporary art, as did the poetry activities themselves. For instance, wrapping a school in paper resembles certain works by Christo, who wrapped a Chicago museum. A poem whitewashed on the street has to be viewed from the air, as did the earthworks of Robert Smithson. Including the public in creating the poem resembled the 1960s "happenings" of Allan Kaprow and others.

The act of writing became the real artwork, the poem being a part of the documentation, along with photographs, films, and videos. Marcel Duchamp and other artists had established the role of documentation in art. Since the poem was a document, I didn't rewrite it after the event. The window opened, the marathon happened, and the window closed. But the objects remained. Usually they were rolls of paper, but sometimes other things. Like art objects, I exhibited these poetry objects—not in museums, but in libraries and bookstores. I transcribed most of them, and published selections in magazines.

The methods I used in my poetry classes grew directly out of my experiences with these marathon events, but there were some differences. For one thing, I started asking students to write directly on objects—bottles, bowls, hand fans, shirts, and other objects—instead of on sheets of paper. Again, my approach had something in common with contemporary art: the Pop artists featured everyday objects in their work, too. Andy Warhol painted soup cans, Jasper Johns depicted American flags, Claes Oldenberg constructed a giant kapoc hamburger.

I didn't consciously model my poetry activities after anyone in particular, but they didn't come flying out of my Alphabet Hat either. They reflect my interests in art and poetry. I like the art of da Vinci, Degas, Picasso, Pollock, and many other artists; and I like the poetry of Shakespeare, Blake, Whitman, William Carlos Williams, Frank O'Hara, and many other poets. Their works have shaped my thinking and influenced my methods.

The Poetry Class for People over Sixty
In 1975 I had the great good fortune to begin teaching a class of older people. Barry Nickelsberg of the Iowa Arts Council contacted me about trying such a project. The Poetry Class for People over Sixty, as the students and I called it, met twice a week for hour-long sessions at the United Methodist Church. We sat around a round table in a room adjacent to the congregate meals lunchroom. I led the meetings and wrote alongside the students.

Each class session loosely followed a structure that evolved over the first few meetings. For the first five to ten minutes, we just talked about anything at all, and we got to know each other. During the next thirty minutes or so, we read our poems from the previous workshop (reproduced on what we called the Poetry Sheet) and discussed them. In the last twenty minutes, we wrote poems, which I later typed up for next meeting.

The students were among the nicest people I've ever known. Because of their willingness to try new ways to make poetry, I learned more about the creative process than ever. They were the first to write poems on mirrors, wood, foam rubber, paper cups and plates, mobiles, and many other objects.

In the first twelve months, we met a little over a hundred times, and we continued meeting for nine more years. Some of the highlights included an incredibly elegant group poetry reading at the University of Iowa's Schambaugh Auditorium, several poetry parties at the students' homes, and four issues of *Speakeasy*, the class magazine. Occasionally I arranged for other artists, including actors and puppeteers, to perform in class as a prelude to writing. Thanks to those students, I made up many of these methods.

Poetry in the Schools
Along with the older people's class, I taught Writers-in-the-Schools programs for five years through the Iowa Arts Council. The Council sponsored my visits to many different sites, including forty or so el-

ementary and junior high schools, a few high schools and junior colleges, a school for the deaf, a hospital, a recreation center, a reformatory, and a retirement home. The response from teachers and students was always positive—with one exception. After my five-day residency in an elementary school, two of the teachers wrote a letter to the Arts Council complaining that I'd told their students that poetry doesn't have to rhyme.

After a couple of years, the Iowa Arts Council became curious about my writing methods. One morning during a residency in Des Moines, a council representative came to the school to observe.

"I was sent here because we heard you were using poker cards in class and that you wrapped a roll of paper around a school. My boss wonders whether you're being serious about teaching poetry."

"Of course I am," I said. "If I weren't, I wouldn't spend time dreaming up these things and trying them out." During class, she listened, took notes, and even played Poetry Poker. Afterwards, she said, "I'm sorry I had to come here, but in a way it's good. My report will show the Arts Council that you are serious and that the students respond well to the methods, which aren't just gimmicks."

"Gimmicks? I hadn't thought about that. Maybe they are, but if so, then a lot of teaching methods are gimmicks!"

Teaching at different schools, institutions, and public settings gave me the chance to sharpen old methods and to invent new ones. I also had the opportunity to see how different ages and types of students responded to poetry in the classroom.

Using This Book

The methods in this book are grouped. Chapters 1 to 3 describe methods using physical objects. Chapters 4 to 7 present methods using linguistic objects—words, phrases, and sentences. Chapter 8 concludes with some inventive student-made methods.

Each method is described in several sections, as shown below. When a section seemed unnecessary, I left it out. With most of the methods, the students write individually for ten to twenty minutes to make one poem. I've noted any exceptions within the text.

Almost all the methods can be used with any age group. In some cases, you might have to make adjustments for students who are too young to write.

The sections are:

Preliminary discussion: introduction to the method.
Description: the way that the students write.
Rules: the way that the students play a game to make a poem.

Materials: writing tools, writing surface, and anything else required to set up the activity.

Preparation: directions for setting up the activity.

Suggested topics: ideas for what to write about, presented as a series of statements and questions that you could offer to the students.

Suggestions: additional information that might add to the activity or help in some way.

Alternative: a possible variation on the activity.

Examples: usually by students.

Illustration: a drawing that you copy for use in the activity.

Word list: a set of words that you copy for use in the activity.

Extra material: additional information that is too long to present in one of the other sections.

Using the Methods in Class

The following three-part approach works for most of the methods. It's flexible enough to be adjusted to most situations.

A. *Preliminary discussion*

1) Talk to the students about how this activity relates to poetry, to language in general, or to the subject of the poem.

B. *Doing the activity*

1) Give directions and suggestions, and answer questions.

2) Distribute the materials, take the students to wherever the writing will take place.

3) Begin writing.

4) Give the students time to make their poems.

5) Have students read or show their poems and talk about them.

C. *Follow-up*

1) Discuss and write about the activity, display the poetry objects, publish the poems in a class magazine or anthology.

The appendices to this book give some slice-of-life views of actual workshops.

CHAPTER 1

PHYSICAL POETRY— PAPER OBJECTS

If all the world were paper,
And all the seas were ink,
And all the trees were bread and cheese,
What should we have to drink?

—Anonymous Traditional Poem

BEFORE reading any further, take out a pencil. Look at the objects near you. Write the word *poetry* on one of them. There. This is probably your first experience since childhood of writing on objects for fun. Children love writing on objects, walls, floors, and hands, but usually they get in trouble for doing it. They learn that paper is the proper place for words. By giving them objects, including paper-made objects, you let them experience the world as a page.

Children aren't the only ones who like putting poems on castles, mirrors, and chopsticks. In fact, as I've noted, senior citizens were the first to try writing on those three objects. They wrote plenty of regular paper-and-pencil poems, too, but writing on objects seemed more adventurous, more liberating.

It is a daring process. When you write on an object, you can't usually rewrite. The raw poem is there, warts and all, for the rest of the class to see. But most of the time the poems turn out well. If they don't, that's OK. Since the poetry activity is presented in the spirit of fun, the poetry doesn't have to be Shakespeare-perfect.

The methods in this section are grouped by the material involved in the activity—paper, wood, paint, food, rubber, rock, glass, styrofoam, and cloth. Many other materials could be used for writing poems, and each would affect the writing process in its own way. For instance, poetry on wood smells, feels, and looks different than poetry on paper.

Like the process, the product is different from what students ordinarily write. The unity of word and picture often create attractive poetry objects.

What objects would your students like to write on?

1. THE TECHNICOLOR PAGE

The Technicolor Page has a vibrant, colorful surface that jumps out at the writer. It's the same length and width as a sheet of typing paper, but it looks and feels different. The slight inclination of the surface gives it a three-dimensionality that your fingers notice when you're writing.

Description
The students write on Technicolor Pages composed of thick pieces of colored posterboard collaged together. Their words can curve and zig-zag in any direction as they climb from color to color.

Materials
scissors
white posterboard (1/8" thick)
colored posterboards (blue, red, yellow, also 1/8" thick)
Elmer's glue or quick-drying glue
black felt-tip pens

Preparation
Cut out a rectangular sheet of white posterboard (8 1/2" x 11") and three pieces of differently colored posterboard. The colored board should be irregularly shaped and in increasingly smaller sizes. Glue all four pieces one on top of the other, with the white board as the bottom layer. Each colored piece should fit completely on the one below it without any overhang.

1) "The shapes are fragments of a broken rainbow. Why is it broken? How can it be fixed?"
2) "The page is a map of a city, a state, or a country. What do the shapes represent?"
3) "These are pieces of a puzzle that can't be assembled. Why not? If it could be, what would it show?"

Alternative
Make the page by gluing three small colored pieces to the white board, but not to each other. Each student writes on one colored piece, then writes across the white board onto another colored piece, and so on, to connect all the colors.

Examples

Over a white page
Shards
fragments
of my planned career
I pick you up and
put you together
and make a
stained glass window

　　—*Pearl Minor, PCPO-Sixty*

1.
Perhaps the garland of flowers
Had on one occasion
Decorated the
Head of a bride

2.
She was beautiful
Wearing all colors of a rainbow
Entwined thru her hair

3.
Now the wreath
Lies silently
On a quaint rocker

4.
The bride
Would carefully
Store her garland
Of flowers.

Perhaps
They will die soon

—Fanny Blair, PCPO-Sixty

The sun shining brightly.
A late August afternoon.
The green plants swaying in the breeze.
The sky above so blue.
With red petunias near.
But God will give me strength
to put the days ahead
to a good purpose
and the rainbow colors intact.

—Nellie Voelckers, PCPO-Sixty

A rainbow is God's promise
That never again would He
Destroy this world
By water or by flood.

The most exciting rainbow
Which I have ever seen
Was really a double rainbow
And rare as a virgin queen.

As we drove past
Half Moon Bay in California
And crossed the bridge
I looked up at the sky.
So blue, so beautiful.
I saw the two rainbows
Arching one below the other.

Lavender and pink.
Lemon yellow and green.
Cerulean blue and orange.
Pale colors on a screen.

The skyline of San Francisco
Beckoned beyond the bridge
And was introduced by the rainbow
For all eternity.
Never shall I forget it
No matter how old I grow to be.

—Alice Gratke, PCPO-Sixty

14

2. POETRY MOBILES

Alexander Calder, the twentieth-century artist, invented the mobile, and it soon became a popular art form around the world. Artists, designers, and teachers have used mobiles in their work without giving its origin a second thought. A mobile's free-floating parts also offer a natural surface for free-floating poetry.

When the older people wrote on mobiles, one of them suggested exhibiting them at the Iowa City Public Library. At the time, I hadn't thought about a community exhibit, but it sounded great. So I called the library and set up a month-long exhibit. The old public library building had eight brick columns separating the card catalogue on the lower entry level from the bookshelves on the first floor. I hung the mobiles between the columns. The effect was magical.

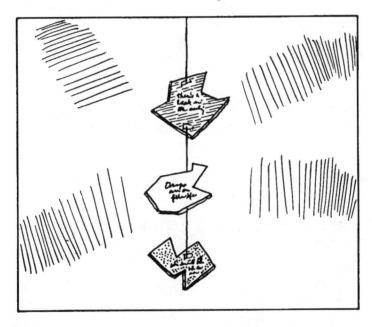

Description
The students write on three-piece Poetry Mobiles—one stanza per side (front and back). When suspended from the ceiling, the pieces spin slowly in the breeze, and the stanzas alternate positions.

Materials
scissors
colored posterboards (blue, red, yellow, 1/8" thick)
clear plastic string or clear fishing line
strapping tape
black felt-tip pens

Preparation

Cut out three irregularly shaped pieces of differently colored posterboard. Lay them one above the other on a table. Connect the top and the middle pieces with a six-inch length of string, and the middle and bottom pieces with another six-inch length. Then tape a length of string to the top of the whole mobile, long enough for suspending it from the ceiling.

Suggested Topics

1) "What does each color and shape suggest to you in terms of objects, feelings, or experiences?"
2) "If this were a machine, how would it work? What would it do? Where would you use it?"

Alternatives

1) The students draw pictures on one side of each piece and write poems on the other.
2) Two students collaborate by writing stanzas on the opposite sides of the mobile pieces. When the pieces turn, their stanzas mesh to change the meanings.
3) After hanging the three pieces from a wooden dowel so they float side by side instead of one above the other, suspend the dowel by a single string, too, so the dowel and the pieces can rotate simultaneously.
4) Make a more complex mobile by using a triangular or wooden frame to hold one or two pieces of posterboard per student. This way all the students have pieces attached to the frame.

Examples

White as driven snow
    in the winter.

The green
    of evergreen trees
    in the Pacific Northwest.

With blue sky
in the background.
    —Louis Taber, PCPO-Sixty

1.
In the garden
blood red beets
growing round

2.
A feeling of envy
not good

3.
Fireflies
shiny on the summer evenings

4.
Blue

The wings of a bluejay

5.
The sky in early morn
Before the day is born

6.
Sliced red apples

  —Nellie Voelckers, PCPO-Sixty

In grade school
I remember
a pretty little girl
singing "My Alice Blue Gown."
She had on a blue dress.

 A
kite
  flying
 like an
 airplane

Blue clouds
 in
    the
      heavens.

White my Sunday
 School dress

Yellow
 sheaves
    of
    oats

The green grass
 of Iowa

  —Julia Kondora, PCPO-Sixty

Leaves
  shine—
      like mobile
sculptures in the sun.
      *
They turn
  in the fall
      *
under
  an
  October
sky.
      *
My mood—
      sometimes!
      *
A
stomach ache
      *
Florida:
  Sunshine factory

   —*Pearl Minor, PCPO-Sixty*

It was smooth—
Looking down
One felt joyful.
Like treading
     on a plush
        carpet.
Another wonder
   of God.
      *
Down, down they come
Soft, fluffy snowflakes
Swirling here and there
A blanket to cover the
           world.
      *
It was a red coat.
How she strutted
Turning round and round.

   —*Fanny Blair, PCPO-Sixty*

3. POETRY CASTLE

In this poetic fantasy, words are the stones that change a box of cardboard into a castle of poetry. The students make a collage of words on the walls, and the resulting lines provide topics and themes for writing on regular paper.

When I brought the Poetry Castle idea into the Poetry Class for People over Sixty, the students were very enthusiastic about it. They took great care to select just the right words to glue to the castle, and they chose just the right place to position them. Some of them were so absorbed that they almost missed lunch in the next room.

A few weeks after the activity, I displayed the castle in the window of a local art supply store, along with poetry objects from two methods discussed below, Poetry Robot and Foam Rubber Poems.

Description
The Poetry Castle sits on a table. Encircling the castle, words and phrases clipped from magazines form a Word Moat. The students pick out words and phrases from the moat and glue them to the castle walls. Then they write poems on paper, mixing words of their own with lines from the castle.

Materials
quick-drying glue
small cardboard boxes
large cardboard box

scissors
white posterboard
colored posterboard (blue)
X-Acto knife
magazines
newspapers
black felt-tip pens
writing paper

Preparation

To construct the castle, glue smaller boxes as turrets to the top corners of the large box that forms the main part of the structure. Cut pieces of white posterboard to fit the sides and tops, and glue them in place. Cut inch-wide strips of blue posterboard (or any color you wish) and glue them around the edges as trimming. Cut windows and a drawbridge into the castle.

To make the moat, cut out words and phrases from magazine and newspaper headlines, and sprinkle them around the castle.

Suggested Topic

"Read over the lines on the castle. Which ones do you like best? What ideas do you get from them? Write a poem with your favorite lines in it."

Alternatives

1) The students bring their own cut-out words for the moat.
2) They build their own smaller buildings out of smaller boxes and cover them with words. When they're finished, they arrange the buildings around the castle to form a kingdom of poetry.

Examples

[COLLAGE LINES]

[On the front wall]

TALKATIVE PICTURE Day
*
the book wrote people
*
SIMULATED
got a bite
*
I make REALITY More? than business
*

Talk How
*

electricity? do it.
*

[SIDE (wrapped around the castle edge)]
*

FREE This BOOK
*

the World Grows A new HOUSE TO PUT A BIG impression
is smoking WITH THE HILL
make Good find the world FULL
first 13 ways

[On the right wall]

From you TO the Pacific
taste."
*

Bridging Business? Problems

Cast of Characters Vanishes
AND THEY travel only on Sundays
to have either a Vacation
or HIDE from the Office
*

AS
*

Barrel of Gaps
*

They Should fuss
OUR NEW CAR:
CRISIS NEARS
*

in
*

you can if you THINK
TRY TO forget ME Dear
*

who ARE You Master OF
*

The perfect week . . . YEAR-ROUND
*

FIND The church
*

Clean dry air

[On the left wall]

Announcing: A CITY OF "MOONLIGHTERS"
thinking Working American Exits and Entrances
the Midway Business SHALL come Along Later
How Could you perform.
*

Look out
A me more than any know
*

FRANKLY We've Been Curious MR. RIGHT
*

Americans AT WAR
News FOR SCHOOLS—
*

love Is my insurance.
DO-IT-YOURSELF
*

Touch THE INVISIBLE
*

Every TIME I SEEK the big success
I lost

[On the back wall]

with the names
*

WORK at IT
*

America's tougher.
*

Giveaway, Babies without RECKONING Parents
it's SOME Game
*

HOW TO smoke cigarette

The King of Canada couldn't drive

A Chapter ON CONSTRUCTIVE writing

READING! about the first BILLION PENSIONS
*

THEY even Asked how I'd know best
*

I AM on A New AM
*

Bring in Their Year
*

spare OUR Novelist

There are some True PHONIES

[On the roof]

She needs SURPRISES
Around the Kitchen
*

losing things less is still good news
But quit KEEPING smoke before you
*

keep OFF
*

How NOW GURUS
*

DON'T PUT up Even One CEILING
NOT ONE

[On the towers]

best
*

IN DEBT
*

Tough
*

open UP about the mouth
*

on RUSH
*

watch life
*

can

Can't
*

you
*

Big Oil's baroque
*

your desk
*
diary
*
BUYING the SUN

   —*Fanny Blair, Alice Gratke, Bea Grimm, Julia Kondora, Dave Morice, Myldred Strong, PCPO-Sixty*

4. THE SQUARE PLANET

The Square Planet gives the students a brave new world to write on and about. The inhabitants of that world would have different problems than people on Earth. The Squarians are geographically divided by six flat sides as well as by the continents. The shape of the planet serves to emphasize how different it is from the earth.

I used the Square Planet as part of a series of activities with first and second graders at Sabin Elementary School in Iowa City. The students made up poems about two characters, Spaceboy and Spacegirl, who take a trip to the Square Planet. Along the way the travelers encounter the Junk King and the Poetry Robot (see the next two methods) and other creatures.

The students dictated their poems to the classroom teacher and to me. Dictation allowed them to express themselves fluidly—too fluidly, perhaps. For every line we wrote down, they spoke, shouted, and laughed at least ten others. At first, I expected the students merely to accept the squareness of the planet and write about extraterrestrial creatures waging battles as in *Star Wars*. Instead, they brought up ways that the shape would affect the lives of the Squarians. This led to discussions of global cooperation, ecology, economics, war, and peace.

After my residency at Sabin, I used the Square Planet exercise in the Poetry Class for People over Sixty, who were delighted to work with the same method as the children.

Description
The students writes short poems (three to six lines) on the surface of the Square Planet—on a continent, an ocean, or an edge. Then, to go into more detail they write another poem on paper.

Materials
glue
tape
cube-shaped cardboard box, measuring at least one foot per side

colored construction paper
black felt-tip pens
writing paper

Preparation
Glue or tape the box shut. Cut six pieces of blue construction paper (representing water) to fit the box and glue them to all six sides. Cut out jagged pieces of colored construction paper (for continents) and glue them to the blue paper, wrapping some of the "continents" around the edges.

Suggested Topic
"What is life like on the Square Planet? How does its shape affect the Squarians? Would people on one side get along with people on the other sides? Would people on different continents (but on the same side) get along? Would the sun shine on some areas more than on others? How would the people travel over the edge?"

Suggestion
Hang the Square Planet from the ceiling, to place it in an orbital display.

Alternative
The students work in small groups. Each group makes its own square planet, star, or moon and writes a collaborative poem on it. Afterward, the entire square solar system can be suspended from the ceiling.

Examples

My First Trip through Space

Now our space capsule blasts off.
We head toward Africa as we go aloft.
Soon we rise higher and higher
Then it is dark and we are not in the view of the sun's fire.
As the sun appears again we also see a square planet.
My pal said, "That planet's a phony I bet.
It must've had a close shave between two other bigger planets.
This way its continents reflect colors.
Its whole appearance is much different than others.
So let's look at it before its corners wear off.
We can tell of this sight and our friends cannot scoff."

—*Cora Pollock, PCPO-Sixty*

Square Planet

Rushing up there
in space without air,

blockhead,
you rock ahead
    tumbling rumbling
    edges crumbling.

Making a din
you try to spin
    thumping
    bumping
rubbing out years
with heat that sears—

And you smash,
and you crash
through the muted music,
through the gentle, lovely music
of the spheres.

        —Pearl Minor, PCPO-Sixty

5. THE JUNK KING

"One person's trash is another person's treasure," the flea-market saying goes. For the Junk King, trash is treasure. He's made of old boxes. His wardrobe recycles the waste of the world, but he couldn't do it without the help of children.

The Junk King was part of the month-long epic of Spaceboy and Spacegirl (see previous exercise). I told my elementary school students that he'd be coming tomorrow, and I asked them to bring some junk to give him. The following day, I brought the Junk King, and they brought the junk. What happened next became the topic of their poetry.

Description
Each student brings a piece of junk from home. At the start of the activity, the students attach their junk to the Junk King using tape, glue, staples, string, or whatever it takes. Then they write poems on colored construction paper, cut them out, and tape them on the king to make a cloak of many colors and words.

Materials
quick-drying glue
cardboard boxes of varying sizes and shapes—one for the head, one for
    the body, two for the arms, two for the legs
acrylic paint

pieces of junk (clean, safe objects)
strapping tape
string
construction paper
scissors
Scotch tape (the "magic transparent" type)
black felt-tip pens

Preparation
Tape all the boxes shut. Using the largest for the body, glue the other boxes onto it to make arms, legs, and head. Then paint a face and other designs on him.

Suggested topics
1) "Why would your piece of trash be treasure for the Junk King? What could he use it for? How much would it be worth to him?"
2) "What could you make out of your junk so it could be useful?"

Alternative
Build two characters, the Junk King and the Junk Queen. Boys and girls bring junk for both potentates and work together decorating them. It would be interesting to see whether gender affected the activity.

6. THE POETRY ROBOT

For the third activity in the word trek of Spaceboy and Spacegirl, I built a Poetry Robot. It was a complicated, time-consuming object to make, but it was well worth the work. I used it in two different classes and displayed it at the public library for five months.

First, I took the robot to the congregate meals site for the Poetry Class for People over Sixty. I arrived early and hid it behind a curtain in the poetry room. Before seeing it, the older people wrote "preview poems" guessing what it looked like. I told them that the Poetry Robot (like the Square Planet of the previous method) was going to be used at Sabin Elementary School, and they were delighted to play an active role. After I brought out the robot and a box of words cut from magazine titles, they glued some of the words to it. Later that day, a friend helped me transport the robot in her car to the school. It was so big I had to hold it out the window by an arm and a leg.

At Sabin, I hid the robot in the janitor's closet until we were ready to begin. The school had open classrooms with four classes sharing the same unpartitioned space. When I brought the robot into the room, the students in my class started playing with it, while students in the other

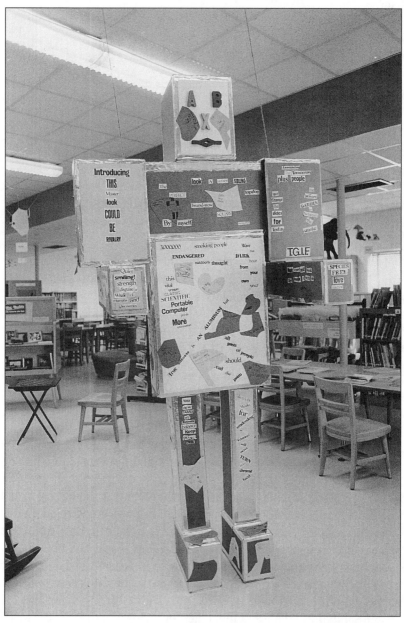

Photo: Dom Franco

classes stared and buzzed with curiosity. Their teachers had to march them past the robot before classes could resume.

The finished robot stayed at the school for two weeks. Then it journeyed to the Iowa City Public Library and lived in the Children's Room for five months. After that, the library gave it a room in the basement. A few months later, when I went to pick it up, it was gone. No one knew where it went, but rumors of a robot muttering poetry and walking the dark alleys of Iowa City abound.

Description
This activity is for two groups of different ages—for instance, a secondary class and a primary class. The older students glue cut-out words to the robot to make lines of poetry, and then they write poems on paper using one or more of the robot's lines.

The next day it's the younger students' turn. They write poems on colored construction paper and glue them to the robot.

Materials
strapping tape
quick-drying glue
12 cardboard boxes of varying sizes
colored posterboard
acrylic paint
magazines
newspapers
colored construction paper
Elmer's glue
black felt-tip pens
writing paper

Preparation
To build the robot, tape the boxes shut and glue them together to make the robot body. Then cut and glue colored posterboard to all sides of it. Seal the seams with strapping tape. Paint or collage a face. Cut out words and phrases from magazine article titles.

Suggestions
1) Have the students write preview poems to guess what the robot looks like.
2) Donate the finished robot to the media center or the library. Include a sign giving credit to the groups who worked on it.
3) Take photos of the students, especially the younger kids. They love to pose with the robot.

Alternative
In addition to the large robot, bring smaller boxes for the students to design, build, and write on their own miniature robots.

Examples
The students in the older people's class wrote the preview poems before seeing the robot. After I brought the robot out, we glued words to make collage lines all over it.

    [PREVIEW POEMS]

    Epitome of Man in Space
    O Strange Configuration.
    You fill me with awe
    And odd foreboding.
    Will future man
    Take on your shape?
    Or are there similar

Giants of your dimensions
In outer space?

    —Benita Allen, PCPO-Sixty

The Robot

I am tall, about six feet.
My body is of cardboard
Covered with a tan sheet.
My face is not too handsome
Because my features are large.
My arms dangle at my side.
Wonder what I can do—

    —Nellie Voelckers, PCPO-Sixty

Jack-o'-Lantern
grinning to its no-ears
seven feet tall
a real "square"
stiff in the joints.
(he should stay out of them)
symphony in pasteboard—
symphony did I say?
His voice has no tone.
See him standing there
leering.

    —Pearl Minor, PCPO-Sixty

    Poetry Robot—
        Cardboard Bard—
The mechanical man
with a computer brain.
He rules society.
Our spiritual ideals
        do not count for anything.
This is a world gone mad
for money & power,
   money and war
      and pleasure.

    —Louis Taber, PCPO-Sixty

[COLLAGE LINES]

[On the chest]

The PERFECT brand-new SQUARE MONSTER
*
look
A writer's SIBLING
*
top dog
*
By myself

[On the stomach]

3,000,000 smoking people
ENDANGERED outdoors thought
*
Wave that DARK hour from your own year
*
this vital UPTIGHT CLASSIC SCIENTIFIC Portable Computer
prints
More information
*
True success is AN ALUMINUM hat
*
all guests or people
should read the prints

[On the right arm]

Introducing THIS Master look COULD BE RIVALRY
*
your office minutes take achieved Programs
*
Quiet smiling!
strength
disguise a Whale of triumphs and discoveries
*
each CONVENTIONAL Shopper's evolution

AMERICAN profit
DO-IT-YOURSELF
*
More than weight

and do something
about your writing
*

twice you said
We're in The advertisement

[On the left arm]

Announcing
The Tomorrow
plus people
*

WHY Change the slides for Today
*

the brilliant GARDEN
in between the smoke
*

T.G.I.F.
*

ARE YOU making GARDEN

write A BOOK INSTEAD
*

much art
started from
READING COLOR
*

SPECIES
FREE
love machine
*

Music travel and book
Give People A wide life

[On the right leg]

Your new FAMILY
with Multimedia balance
Keep people FREE
*

Problems of the FUTURE
can be less today

[On the left leg]

electricity Works
for underdog
Because Technology will never TURN into
chrome Food:

[On the back]

Books Guide
pictures find ways
Now find 'em
*
CAMERA PRINTS
can make Easy money
*
Smokey quit Polar rights Expedition
*
the $500 new pictures
must CAMP for three PAPERS

[On the right side]

the illustrated MATHEMATICAL GAMES
produce less opportunities
*
Could one guide the way
to a Special man

[On the left side]

Edition Reports
highway conflicts
of cars Pony
*
we can Get
city Jobs

> —*Benita Allen, Fanny Blair, Gladys Edwards, Pearl Minor, Dave Morice, Cora Pollock, with visitors Barry Nickelsberg and Michelle Kulefesky, PCPO-Sixty*

7. AUTUMN LEAF POEMS

One fall I saw some paper autumn leaves on sale at Walgreen's. I bought some and took them to class the next day. It was almost as if they were designed for inspiring a simple seasonal verse.

Description
The students write short poems (four to eight lines) on two paper autumn leaves, one large and one small.

Materials
two paper autumn leaves (5" wide and 3" wide)
black felt-tip pens

Suggested Topics
1) "On the large leaf, tell about the leaf. Why did it fall? Where did it land? What kind of day was it when the leaf fell? What colors are the leaves on the ground? When did they fall?"
2) "On the small leaf, tell about the tree it fell from. What kind of tree is it? What does it look like? What colors are the leaves still on the tree? When will they fall?"

Suggestions
1) If you can't locate any paper leaves at the store, ask the students to make them. You'll get a lot more sizes and shapes.

2) Find a branch with lots of smaller branches and tape up the finished leaf poems for display.

Examples

In these examples, the words on the large leaf appear before the asterisk, and those on the small leaf come after it.

The days have become cool & chilly.
Autumn time has come at last.
The place is neither flat nor hilly.
The summer time is now long past.
The leaves have turned from green
To colors of a different sheen:
Beautiful reds, oranges, & yellows.
                    *
I came from a tall oak
Beside the rilly brook.
The different colors that I look
May be found in a book.

                —*Nellie Voelckers, PCPO-Sixty*

Down down
They tumble
To the ground.
Day after day
During the heat
Of summer
They shaded
The earth below.

Now gusty winds
Are fast at work.
First one leaf
And then
Many leaves
Follow
The leader.

All is
Quiet now.
Leaves are nestled
Together.
Quietness reigns.
Take care
And God bless.
                    *

One leaf remains at the top of a venerable oak tree.
His time is near—go now—Adieu.

—Fanny Blair, PCPO-Sixty

A paper leaf you say?
Well aren't trees really paper
Eventually?

This gaily colored paper leaf
Is not brighter than a real one.
What a lift to the heart
Is a grove of golden maples
Late in the fall.
*
Even green leaves
Are a delight
When spring arrives
After winter's dreariness.

—Alice Gratke, PCPO-Sixty

8. VERSE TUBES

English is written from left to right and then down. Other languages go in other directions. Writers in all languages have always done one thing the same: they've written on a flat surface. Even the Sumerians, thought to be the first users of language, carved their letters into flat clay tablets. The Egyptians wrote on flat paper that was rolled into scrolls for storage and slowly unrolled by hand for reading. For some reason, the inventive Egyptians never built a speedy mechanical scrolling device during all the centuries that they used scrolls. In this exercise, the surface is a tube used for composing a poem in one line that winds it around like the stripes on a barber pole.

Description
Everyone writes a poem on a cardboard tube, with the words spiraling downward or upward from one end to the other.

Materials
empty paper towel rolls (or other cardboard tubes)
black felt-tip pens

Suggested Topic
"A lot of things revolve or spin or go around in circles. You could probably list ten in a couple of minutes. Just pick three or four of them. How
are they alike, and how are they different?"

Alternatives
1) When the line reaches the end of the tube, the student turns it upside
down and continues writing the line in the other direction till returning
to the starting word.
2) Use a tube that is one foot wide or more. A sturdy cardboard moving
barrel is ideal. The student writes a single line all the way around until
it touches itself.

9. VERSE LOOP

This simple but effective activity lets the students get wrapped up in a
poem. It's good to have the students sitting on the floor, and it's even
better to have them outside sitting on the grass.

Description
Each student wears a wide loop of paper like a life preserver while writing a poem anywhere on it.

Materials
scissors
roll of paper (12" wide)
tape
colored felt-tip pens

Preparation
For each loop, cut a length of paper four feet long and tape the ends together.

Suggested Topics
1) "Look all around you in a complete circle. Now, without looking
again, write about what you saw."
2) "One of the most important inventions in history is the wheel. How
do you think it was invented? What was it used for? Can you think of a
new use for the wheel?"

10. MOEBIUS STRIP POEM

The Moebius strip is a wonder of mathematical nature. At first glance,
it appears to have two surfaces like an ordinary sheet of paper. But if

you draw a continuous line down the strip, eventually you travel to the other side and then back again, ending up where you started. The strip seems to defy logic, and it challenges students to write on a surface that isn't what it seems.

Description
Each student writes a one-line poem on a Moebius strip until the line winds back around to the beginning word.

Materials
scissors
white drawing paper (24" long)
Elmer's glue
black felt-tip pens

Preparation
Cut a strip of paper measuring 1" x 24", grasp it by the ends, and twist one end 180 degrees. Bring the ends together and glue them.

Suggested Topics
1) "For good or for bad, life takes unexpected turns. Just when you think something will happen one way, it happens the opposite way. Write about an unexpected turn in your life."
2) "The Moebius strip is just a piece of paper, but its effect can seem almost magical. Have you ever seen anyone perform a magic trick? What was it? Do you know how it was done?"
3) "Write a message to yourself—a reminder, a promise, a wish, or a secret."

Example

[Written as a single line]

"One day I wrote
myself a note.
My self wrote back instead
another note
just like my note
and this is what it said:

•

Strange Twists in the Moebius Strip

Paper loops have other surprising properties you can demonstrate in a topological magic show. When you cut a simple loop (no twists) down the centerline, you get two simple loops the same size and half the width of the original. That's what you'd expect.

But try making three different kinds of Moebius strips by twisting the paper once, twice, and three times, 180 degrees per twist. When you cut them down the centerline, what do you get?

One twist—a twisted circle twice the diameter. Two twists—two twisted circles linked like a chain. Three twists—a circle twice the diameter with a knot tied in it.

11. POETRY SIGNS

A few decades ago, the Burma Shave company put rhyming advertisements on roadside signs. Passing a set of them, the driver could read the phrases of the poem over a stretch of 200 or 300 feet. The effect of time between the signs built up the tension of the words. Burma Shave signs are a thing of the past, but the company's innovative way of presenting verse can be adapted for current use.

Description

Students in groups of four write collaborative poems in round-robin fashion. That is, instead of a single sheet of paper going around, the four students start poems on separate sheets and pass them around after writing each line. When everyone has written a line of each poem, the poems are done. Then the group picks one of the poems to write on four Poetry Signs, one line per sign. The students take the signs outside and stick them along the sidewalk at three- or four-foot intervals.

Materials
scissors
colored posterboard (18" x 24")
strong stapler
wooden poles (4' long)
quick-drying glue
wide and thin black felt-tip pens
writing paper

Preparation
Cut out 9" x 12" rectangles of posterboard. For each sign, glue two rect-angles back to back with one end of a pole sandwiched between them. Staple together for reinforcement.

Suggested Topics
1) "Most street signs say predictable things: STOP, YIELD, NO PARK-ING. Think of a message that you wouldn't expect to see on a street sign. What does it say? How would people react to it?"
2) "Signs have their good and bad points. What is the best thing about a sign? What is the worst?"
3) "If a sign could talk, what would it say to the person reading it?"

Alternatives
1) The students write directly on the signs.
2) Each student writes individually, either on a single sign or stringing his or her poem out over four signs.
3) Same as above, but each student makes a drawing related to the poem on the other side of the sign.
4) To cut down on the number of signs, the students pair up to put one poem on one side and one on the other.

12. POETRY PICNIC

At a Special Populations Art Festival, students with physical disabilities wrote and drew on drawings of plates and cups. Originally, the activity was going to be a table poem—just a long sheet of paper taped across the tops of several tables. During the set-up, however, the paper looked empty, so I suggested to my assistants that we draw table settings on the paper.

A few weeks later, the students in the Poetry Class for People over Sixty wrote on paper cups and plates. For that activity, I put pieces of paper containing related phrases and topics in the cups and on the plates; for example, "cup of boats," "cup of trains," and "plate of clouds," "plate of mountains."

Description
The students write poems and draw pictures on a paper plate and a paper cup. When they're finished writing, they get a real snack and a real drink—in new cups and plates, of course.

Materials
tables
paper plates
paper cups
watercolor pens with potable ink

Preparation
Set the table with a cup, a plate, two or three watercolor pens, and, if needed, a plastic fork and spoon for each student.

Suggested Topics
1) "Think about your favorite food, what it looks like, how it smells, feels, and tastes. Imagine taking a bite. How can you describe something so delicious in words?"
2) "Before we serve the snack and the drink, what do you think you'll get? What do you hope you'll get?"

Alternative
Put pieces of paper with phrases on them. Sample phrases: "cup of boats," "cup of cars," "plate of clouds," "plate of rivers."

Examples
For the first two poems, the students wrote on drawings of plates on a large sheet of paper that served as a tablecloth.

Have a Piece of My Pizza

Have a piece of my pizza—
it will make you smell like onions, olives, tomatoes—
covered with cheese and saucy like sausages.
Pizza is the core of my Personality!
You don't like pizza—you don't like me.

—Anonymous student, Special Populations Art Festival, Iowa City

Upon the Blue Plate

Upon the blue plate
    fried chicken.
And you know what they
    say . . . you got to
eat a little chicken
every single day
or you may go astray
I think you'd better
    stay and have
a bit before you
    leave

—Anonymous student, Special Populations Art Festival, Iowa City

(The rest of the poems follow the directions in the alternative. The titles refer to the phrases in the cups and plates.)

Plate of Mountains

Quickly now we
approach a plate of
mountains—what a
sight—all bicycles
keep to the right. Zoom
zoom—up & down the
sides of the mountains
the riders disappear—
They are lost in a
cloud of dust

—Fanny Blair, PCPO-Sixty

Plate of Rivers

As the cup of boats
Passed over the plate of rivers,
A red boat splashed down

On the Blue River.
As it moved down the stream
It disappeared under an arbor of trees.
The orange boat fell into the foam below Emerald River falls.
After the silver boat found a place in the golden light of the setting sun
    on Pacific River,
All the other boats found rivers on which to spend the night,
As they twinkled and sparkled about their delightful travels of the day.

—*Cora Pollack, PCPO-Sixty*

Cup of Boats

A cup of boats
Floated thru the air
Spilling blue and green
As well as ocean foam

—*Cora Pollock, PCPO-Sixty*

13. CALENDAR POEM

"Tomorrow and tomorrow and tomorrow / Creeps in this petty pace from day to day," and the students can write a slow-motion poem on a calendar page to emphasize the point. The grid of dates calls attention to the passing days and slows down the reading of the poem. This activity was designed after a cartoon version of Macbeth's "Tomorrow" soliloquy.

Description
The student writes a poem and draws pictures (of faces, footprints, stick people, anything) on a calendar page. Each date-square gets one to three words and a drawing.

Materials
calendar
photocopy machine
black felt-tip pens

Preparation
Make photocopies of the calendar pages.

Suggested Topics
1) "What makes time go fast for you? What makes it go slow?"
2) "If time were an animal, what kind would it be? What would it do to pass the time?"
3) "Write a poem for any holiday listed on your calendar page."

IOWA STATE BANK & TRUST COMPANY

Serving the banking needs of your community for over 50 years

Iowa City and Coralville   Member FDIC

Main Bank:
102 S. Clinton/356-5800

Clinton St. Office:
325 S. Clinton/356-5960

Keokuk St. Office:
Keokuk St. & Hwy, 6 Bypass/356-5970

Rochester Ave. Office:
2233 Rochester Ave./356-5990

Coralville Office:
110 First Ave./356-5990

DECEMBER

SUN	MON	TUE	WED	THU	FRI	SAT
			ISB&T	1 TOMORROW,	2 AND TOMORROW,	3 AND TOMORROW.
		Happy Holidays!				
4 CREEPS IN THIS	5 PETTY PACE	6 FROM DAY	7 TO DAY,	8 TO THE LAST SYLLABLE	9 OF RECORDED TIME;	10 AND ALL OUR
11 YESTERDAYS	12 HAVE LIGHTED FOOLS	13 THE WAY TO DUSTY DEATH.	14 OUT, OUT, BRIEF CANDLE!	15 LIFE'S BUT	16 A WALKING SHADOW,	17 A POOR PLAYER
18 THAT STRUTS AND FRETS	19 HIS HOUR	20 UPON THE STAGE,	21 AND THEN IS HEARD	22 NO MORE;	23 IT IS	24 A TALE
25 TOLD BY	26 AN IDIOT,	27 FULL OF	28 SOUND	29 AND FURY,	30 SIGNIFYING	31 NOTHING.

Thanks to the ISB&T for the use of this page.

BY WILLIAM SHAKESPEARE

4) "Write about your birthday or someone else's. If you want the calendar page for a particular month, just ask for it."
5) "Make up your own holiday. What is it called? What is the date? How do you celebrate it?"

14. POSTAGE STAMP POEMS

Young philatelists will appreciate this activity. The challenge is to write as small as possible on the back of a used postage stamp. Who can write the most lines? Are they legible?

Stamp collecting has been around ever since the first postage stamps were printed a couple of hundred years ago. Collectors enjoy the beauty, the romance, and the history behind them. As I learned at a fourth and fifth grade hobby festival, stamp collecting is one of the four most popular things to collect at that age. The others include trading cards, comic books, and coins.

Description
Each student picks a postage stamp from a pile of stamps and write poems in tiny letters on the back.

Materials
100 or more used postage stamps from around the world
very sharp pencils

Suggested Topics
1) "What is shown on the front of your stamp? How would you describe it in a few words? Why do you think it was put on the stamp?"
2) "You want to send a secret message written on the back of a stamp. What is the message? Who will receive it?"

Suggestion
Get two copies of each stamp to use for a display. Mount the picture side of one next to the poem side of its duplicate. (Ask any stamp-collecting student for suggestions and help with obtaining the stamps.)

Alternatives
1) The student selects more than one stamp and writes one stanza on each.
2) Using uncancelled stamps with people's faces on them, each student glues two stamps to an envelope and writes a conversation between the two people, putting their words in cartoon balloons. The student can then draw bodies to go with the heads.

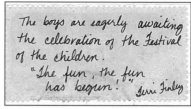

15. POEM IN A BOTTLE

Shipwrecked sailors have written messages on small pieces of paper, stuffed them in bottles, and tossed them into the ocean in the hopes of getting rescued. Armchair sailors build model ships within bottles and display them in their dens. Students can do both by writing poems and putting them in bottles.

Description
Each student cuts out three pieces of differently colored construction paper. The shapes can resemble ships, islands, anchors, treasure chests, and other nautical things, or nothing in particular. Then he or she writes on all three pieces and stuffs them into a bottle.

Materials

scissors
colored construction paper
glass or plastic bottles (from quart to gallon size)
black felt-tip pens

Suggested Topics

1) "You're shipwrecked on a desert island. A bottle floats in on the tide. You write a message on a piece of paper, slip it into the bottle, and toss the bottle back into the waves. What was the message?"
2) "Instead of sending an SOS, you decide you like the island and you plan on staying a long time. You build a ship in the bottle to remember what your own ship looked like. What was the name of the ship? How did it get shipwrecked? Why do you like the island?"
3) "You've found a buried treasure on the island. What is it? Where was it buried? Who buried it? What will you do with it?"
4) "You write a message in the bottle for people to find in the future. What do you tell them?"

Suggestion

Bring sand and seashells for the students to put in the bottles with their poems, and ask the students to bring bottles of their choice.

Examples

The stanzas below, marked off by asterisks, appear on separate pieces of construction paper in the bottle.

Message to the Future

Hello! Out there!
Are your homes as warm
as your hearts?
How do you travel and
    where
do your dreams take you?
In our time the future
                *
was looking grim.
Prospects were pretty slim
for enduring peace. In the
    East
fighting continued. The beast
    moved toward Bethlehem
                *
After all these years
    man must have learned

to keep from being
    burned
by greed, extravagance,
    war.
You must open a
    bright new door!

        —Pearl Minor, PCPO-Sixty

I Was on a Beautiful Ship

I was on a beautiful ship
enjoying a vacation
suddenly a derelict ship
with criminals came alongside
and boarded the ship
We were transferred aboard this ship
It was not a seaworthy ship
and it sunk near an Island.
            *
This Island was beautiful
Monkeys chattered, birds flew
The banana trees were full of fruit
We found roots for vegetables
            *
We found a map in a jar
Saying there was treasure to be found.
We followed directions
and found the treasure
Life-giving water from a cool spring

        —Julia Kondora, PCPO-Sixty

16. ROLODEX POEM

The Rolodex is an ingenious mechanical device for holding file cards on a circular axis. It carries at least 1,000 cards, and is available in different sizes (with different-sized cards) through office supply stores. It's perfect for a year-long random access collaborative poem.

During the school year, students write short lines on one or more cards at any locations in the file. They can read the poems in their free time, flipping from card to card in any order.

Description
The students write about whatever they want on the cards in a Rolodex. After the introductory writing, they can add lines and read the poem in

their free time throughout the school year. The poem continues year after year with each new group of students, and it ends when every card on the Rolodex has something on it.

Materials
Rolodex cardfile
file cards
felt-tip pens

Suggested Topic
"To start, pick an object in the room and write about it. After today, you can add more words and lines on any topic to the Rolodex during your free time."

17. THUMB-BOOK POEM

The tiny pages of a thumb-book are no bigger than a butterfly's wing, yet they can contain a poem appearing one word per page, a secret poem whose meaning is known only to the poet.

Description
Each student makes a thumbprint on the front cover of a tiny blank book. Then he or she writes a secret poem in it, one word per page. There are no sentences, just key words that remind the writer of the secret but give it away to no one else.

Materials
scissors
white typing paper
colored typing paper
stapler

black stamp pads
black felt-tip pens
writing paper

Preparation
Cut out pages (1" square) from white paper and a cover (1" x 2") from colored paper. Wrap the cover around the pages, and staple once along the spine.

18. BOOK WITH A HUNDRED-FOOT PAGE

In sharp contrast to the thumb-book, this book's last page unrolls and keeps unrolling beyond the length of the classroom. It's an ongoing project that begins with everyone writing in it.

I first tried this activity in a different form at Thomas Jefferson College in Philadelphia. On a sunny day in the commons, I wrote a poem incorporating words and comments by students, teachers, and others. After putting something on every page, I unrolled the final page out to its full hundred feet and worked my way down it. On reaching the end, I curved the line around and continued back to the beginning.

About twenty feet from completion, it started raining. I raced to write the final words. Luckily, the book dried with no major damage. The English professor who'd arranged for my visit borrowed it and displayed it in a glass case in one of the halls for a month.

Description
The students begin the activity by writing words, lines, and poems on the hundred-foot page. After that, they add to the long page and to the regular pages throughout the year.

Materials
blank book
yardstick
roll of white paper (100' long x height of the pages in the blank book)
black felt-tip pens
scissors
wooden dowel rod (3/4" diameter x height of the book)
handsaw
Elmer's glue
strapping tape

Preparation
Measure the roll of paper and mark the edge at every ten feet. Cut it at one hundred feet. If the paper is too wide for the book, trim it along the edge. Glue the beginning of the long page to the inside back cover of the blank book, and tape the other end of it to the pole. Scroll the page around the dowel rod.

Suggested Topic
"Writing on such a long page is like going on a journey. Where will the page take you? What will you encounter along the way?"

Example
This is the final stretch of the hundred-foot page in the Philadelphia book. The words go in a line that curves up and down all the way to the end.

... A tarnished coin in his pocket will buy him a ride on the orange Ferris wheel at dusk. He'll victoriously circle the atmosphere around his forehead. In his memory, the pyramids send letters to the ancients. The knowledge fits into thousands of microscopes. It is enlarged beyond belief. The rain starts to fall on the bench. The droplets blur the intricacies of these medicinal syllables. Faster and faster: a literal race against time and water. We won!

19. INKBLOT POEMS

Thanks to Dr. Hermann Rorschach, the inkblot has been an endless source of fascination for psychiatrists. It also can be used in other creative fields, when shapes stimulate the imagination instead of the id.

Description
Each student folds a sheet of paper in half, opens it, pours a few drops of ink on it, and folds it back up. Then he or she opens it up again to reveal the inkblot and writes about it on the unblotted area.

Materials
white drawing paper
India ink
eyedropper
black felt-tip pens

Suggested Topic
"What do you see in the inkblot? Any faces, people, animals, buildings, or other objects? What are they doing? Where is this scene taking place?"

Suggestion
The students make color blots with acrylic paint. (American artist Man Ray did a series of paintings using this method.)

Examples

The Flower Pot

The flower pot said
Why am I black
when I should be green
Why do I have black
leaves when they
should be green,
maybe it's fall

and my leaves
are dying.

—*Clarice Stenby, PCPO-Sixty*

The All-Black Butterfly

Two eyes glare
The butterfly hovers
In the air
Above the clovers
Where are the colors
Oh! this is a new butterfly bred
Minus the yellow blue & red
To make man wonder—
What next?

—*Nellie Voelckers, PCPO-Sixty*

The headless wonder!
*
Bend your back, lady.
*
Eyes in a cow's head.
*
Legless beauty (!)
*
Eyes between the horns
*
Boxing gloves
*
Twin
*
Siamese twin heads
Joined at the nose.
*
Get me a wheelchair

—*Pearl Minor, PCPO-Sixty*

20. INKSPLASH POEMS

This activity harnesses the force of gravity to set up the poem. Ink splashes like rain. Watching the splashes is fascinating enough, but writing words around the splashes is even more intriguing.

Description
Fill an eyedropper with black ink and hold it over a large white sheet of paper taped to the floor. Slowly, as students watch, squeeze out drops of ink and aim them so that they scatter across the surface. The students sit or kneel around the paper and write poems on it. Their words can travel around the ink or go through it, and they can cross over each other's lines.

Materials
white paper (36" x 12')
masking tape
black felt-tip pens
washable black ink
eyedropper

Preparation
Unroll the paper on the floor and tape it down with a piece of masking tape every foot or so around the perimeter.

Suggested Topic
"What did the splashes look like when they fell and hit the paper? What do they look like now? As you write on the paper, let your words talk about the shapes they pass."

Suggestions
1) After the poems are written, squeeze a few more drops on the paper. The ink will splatter around the words for an interesting effect.
2) If time and space permits, let the students squeeze out the ink. Each student begins writing at his or her own splash.
3) Use different colors for the splashing and writing.

21. SHADOW POEMS

One student writes on another student's shadow. This shady activity is based on shadow figures that hands can make—people, animals, monsters, or mystery creatures. Without any practice at all, anyone can make a shape.

Description
One student makes a shadow figure on the paper and holds it in place. The other student writes a poem about it on the shadow. After writing the poem, the second student makes the shadow and the first writes a poem about it on the shadow.

Suggested Topics
1) "What creature casts such a shadow? Describe what it looks like, where it lives, and what it does all day. You can write about a real creature or an imaginary one."
2) "Pretend that shadows have lives of their own. What do they do at night? Where do they go? How do they feel about us? What are their names?"

Alternative
Instead of making a shadow figure with the hand, each student writes on the silhouette of a face or the shadow cast by an object.

22. POETRY DOLLARS

In my Introduction to Children's Literature class at the University of Iowa, I discussed a variety of poetry writing methods for use in elementary schools, and I asked my students to try the following exercise. Their poems seemed to fall into a few broad categories: concerns about personal finances; political statements about taxes and the budget; moral comments about "filthy" money; and funny lines about shopping. One student asked her son, Daniel, to do the activity, and it worked very well. He made a surprisingly (and perhaps unintentionally) political statement.

U.S. paper money is a timely issue, more so than usual. The government may soon be changing the designs of the greenback. It's become one of the easiest currencies of the world to counterfeit. The culprits range from office workers at the color copier to an unfriendly foreign government with an American printing press.

In any case, our paper money could use a change. This activity gives students the chance to make up their own designs.

Description
Each student draws a new design for paper money on one side of a "blank" dollar and writes a poem on the other side.

Materials
white cardstock
scissors
colored felt-tip pens
art supplies (crayons, watercolors, acrylic paints, colored pencils, etc.)

Preparation
Cut cardstock to the size of a dollar bill.

Suggested Topics
1) "Our paper money may be redesigned in the next few years. What do you think it will look like? Draw your own design for the U.S. dollar on one side, and write a poem about the design or about money on the other."
2) "Draw a design for an imaginary country on one side, and write a poem about the country on the other. What is the name of the country? How big is it? What do they make or grow to sell?"

Suggestion
Show the students examples of paper money from foreign countries. To order a supply, here are two sources selling sets of different world banknotes, with their current prices:

Smith
PO Box 904
Crowley, TX 76036
12 for $2, 25 for $5, 50 for $10

Murray
Box 373-CW
Pell Lake, WI 53157
50 for $9.75, 100 for $25

Examples

I like it

(Moby Dick is
the president—
the other fish
are soldiers)

—Daniel, fourth grade

Money is like honey.
You could eat honey until
you drop or you could
spend money until you drop!
Money is like honey.

—Jena Hankemeier, undergraduate

Somewhere over
the rainbow
Is where money
seems to be
When one is a
student
And has to pay
the University
fee!

—Diane Spicknall, undergraduate

•

The Money Artist and the Secret Service

London artist J. S. G. Boggs makes money by drawing it. In the worlds of art and coin collecting, he's known as a "money artist." In the world of crime, he's known as a "con artist." He draws paper money and spends it.

Boggs is a gifted artist who has chosen money as the focus of his artistic career. When he's in a country, he sketches pictures of its currency and uses it to shop at expensive stores or eat at fancy restaurants. His drawings aren't exact copies. They may include a different building or a different legend.

Before spending his bills, Boggs tells people that he's an artist and his money is his art. His work is so good, that many people are happy to accept it in place of the real thing. And they're wise to do so: as artworks, most of Boggs's bills are worth more to collectors than the bills they depict.

Where in the world did he get the idea in the first place? On a visit to Chicago in 1984 he wandered into a restaurant and ordered a doughnut and a bottomless cup of coffee. All he had was a dollar. While sipping the coffee, he sketched the dollar on a napkin. The waitress came up to the table and said, "Why, I think that is the most beautiful $1 bill I have ever seen. I'd like to have that." Boggs was surprised, even angered, that she should want something that he spent time on. He refused to give it to her. She offered him $20. No, he said. $40. No. Disappointed, she walked away and continued working.

Boggs started having second thoughts. As he tells it, "Here I have been struggling all of my life to find somebody who would appreciate my art in the way that I appreciate it, and here is this soul that does, and what do I do, I rebuff her." He asked for the check. When she gave it to him, he offered to pay for it with the napkin. She joyfully accepted the "money" and gave him a real dime in change. He framed it.

Since then, he's drawn British pounds, Swiss francs, and other currencies of the world. In some places, his work gets questioned by the law; in other places, it doesn't. No country has tracked the career of J. S. G. Boggs more vigorously than the United States. A few years ago, Secret Service agents confiscated examples of Boggs's artwork and his collection of dollar bill images on objects. The U.S. government has since required that any catalogues of his work reproduce it according to the regulations for reproducing regular U.S. paper money.

Boggs hasn't been arrested yet. He's become too well known as an artist. He's the only person in the world who can draw up his own funds on the spot.

23. POETRY COMICS

Poems and cartoons might seem to make an odd couple, yet all through history—and even earlier—words and pictures have appeared side by side. In certain ancient languages, such as Egyptian and Chinese, some words *are* pictures, and vice versa. Children experience both words and pictures in picture books. As children get older, however, the number of pictures in their books decreases. By adulthood, pictures are eliminated from nearly all novels. But the word-picture connection thrives in one genre popular with all ages—the comic book.

In creating poetry comics, the students connect the two forms of expression in a format familiar to them. Because most students have pleasant associations with comic books, they quickly warm to the idea. The main activity uses a cartoon version of "I Wandered Lonely as a Cloud" by William Wordsworth. However, there are many other approaches that work, too, and some of them are discussed in the Alternatives section.

Description
Read Wordsworth's "I Wandered Lonely as a Cloud" to the students, then hand out copies of the cartoon version to show how pictures affect the meaning of the words. Each student writes a poem and makes it into a cartoon.

Materials
writing paper
white drawing paper
black felt-tip pens
cartoon version of Wordsworth's poem (see figure)

Suggested Topic
"Suppose you were wandering around all alone. What animal or object would you be? Write a poem starting with, 'I wandered lonely as a . . .,' and then draw a cartoon of it. If you want, you can use a different feeling instead of loneliness."

Alternatives
1) Use a different well-known poem as a model for the writing. You don't have to present it in cartoon form.

I wandered lifeless as a rock,
That was stiff and rugged;

When all at once I herd
some children I could hear my heart
pumping;

Then I felt like jumping.

—*Gary Milder*

—*Kristi Davis*

—*Pearl Minor*

2) Don't use a model poem. You might suggest topics that reflect the characters, settings, and plots in the major types of comic books—superhero, sci-fi, mystery, modern romance, cowboy, funny animals. For instance, the superhero might be introduced like this: "You discover that you have a superpower. What is this power? How did you get it? What will you do with it?"

The process of writing and drawing can be combined in a number of ways:

> 1) Write-draw: Write a poem, draw a cartoon with the poem's words in it.
> 2) Write-exchange-draw: Write a poem, exchange poems with another student, draw a cartoon with the other student's words in it.
> 3) Draw-write.
> 4) Draw-exchange-write.

For more suggestions and examples, see my books *Poetry Comics* and *How to Make Poetry Comics*.

Examples

The poems below appeared in *Poetry Comics No. 9*, a magazine that I produced. They came from about 120 poems by as many fourth–seventh graders I taught during several Poets-in-the-Schools residencies. The students also drew cartoon illustrations to accompany their writing.

I Wander Lonely as a Water Balloon

I wander lonely as a water balloon. Trying to find a target. Quickly falling from the top of a building. I pick up speed as I fall. Going faster ever faster. Falling into an endless void. Faster, gaining speed every second. Faster, faster, faster. Everything is blurry. Splat!

> —*Robert Johnston, seventh grade*

I wandered lonely as a pig
and I told him to do the jig
while the pig was doing the jig
I told him to dig and he dug.

> —*Melody, fourth grade*

Wandering Paper

One day I was walking,
And I heard a tiny scream,
And I saw a paper floating down toward me.
It had eyes, legs, ears, nose, just like me.

But as it touched the ground it ran away

—Katie, seventh grade

I wander as if I'm a rock.

I feel like I'm not I got everything I should.

—Herby Arreola, fourth grade

A Blue Crayon

As I wandered through
the timber feeling like a
blue crayon.
I was down in the blues.
And this is how it happened.
I was on the telephone,
talking to one of my friends,
because I was about to stay
overnight with her.
When my mom said to me,
We are going to the timber to
have a picnic for a family
reunion. I told my friend
and she said it's OK.
Aw—! I said. Do we have to go!
Yes! mom said. We have to go!
So now I am wandering
through the timber feeling
like a blue crayon, down in
the blues.

—Kelli Heindel, seventh grade

Wandering

Wandering down the highway
There is not a car in sight.
It is midnight and I'm all alone.
The moon is clear and very bright.

Absence is near I have no one to talk to
For I have no friends.
The highway is never ending,
For all it has is bends.

—Doug Czerniakowski, seventh grade

I Wandered Lonely as a Flea

I wandered lonely as a flea,
Hoping someday I would
return home,
It's very lonely as a flea.
You never know where you
will be.
The jungle of hair is all
you see.
In the life of a flea.
I hope someday to be
something besides a flea.

—*Paula Leinbach, seventh grade*

24. FILL-IN-THE-BALLOONS CARTOON PAGE

Empty cartoon balloons seem to demand words. After all, the comic book panels still have characters, setting, and action, but without words the meaning can be puzzling. The students write their own words and follow this up with a narrative poem to expand the comic book story.

Description

Each student writes words in the empty cartoon balloons on a specially prepared comic book page, clarifying what is going on in the cartoon. Then he or she writes a narrative poem based on the cartoon.

Materials

comic books in several genres (e.g., superhero, funny animal, romance, western, supernatural, and detective)
scissors
typing paper
Elmer's glue
white correction fluid ("white-out")
photocopy machine and white paper
black felt-tip pens

Preparation

Cut out 15–20 panels from a comic book story and "white out" the words. Arrange a few panels in the 8 1/2" x 11" position on a copy machine and copy them, to make one page. Make additional pages by rearranging the panels and by switching them with other panels. Mix in panels from other comic book genres, too. Make enough for all the students to have different pages.

Suggestion
Assemble a poetry comic book with the students' comic book pages and narrative poems on facing pages. Together, decide on a name for the book and its cover design. Publish a photocopy edition and distribute copies to the class.

Alternatives
1) Bring a box of individual panels and ask the students to design the pages. Then photocopy those pages and hand them out.
2) The students in a small group collaborate on a four- to five-page comic book and poem.
3) Use newspaper comic strip panels for the pages.

25. MR. & MS. POETRYHEAD

Remember the days when Mr. Potatohead was made from a real potato? Now he's made of plastic to avoid the mess. Mr. and Ms. Poetryhead are made of paper, and their lighthearted shapes provide funny surfaces for funny poetry.

Description
Each student glues colorful features—eyes, ears, nose, etc.—to an oval base to make Mr. or Ms. Poetryhead. Then everyone writes a poem on all the different parts. No matter what the topic, it should be guided by topsy-turvy logic.

Materials
scissors
colored posterboards (blue, red, yellow)
glue
black felt-tip pens

Preparation
Cut out an oval piece of posterboard (about 6" x 10") for the head and smaller pieces for eyes, ears, nose, mouth, eyebrows, hair, beard, and mustache. Make more than enough for all the students so they have lots of choices.

Suggested Topic
"Mr. and Ms. Poetryhead write poetry on their faces, but what they write is crazy nonsense. In their world, dogs meow under a green grass sky while they eat dinner on the roof of their house. They bring trash inside instead of throwing it out. They laugh instead of cry, and they cry instead of laugh. What does your Poetryhead write?"

Suggestions
1) Instead of providing pieces, let the students cut out eyes, ears, etc., in the shapes and colors of their choice.
2) The students cut out a larger piece of posterboard to make a body, tape the head to it, and write on both head and body.

•

The Stupids Get Censored

The Stupids are possibly the most absurd family in all children's literature. They star in a series of picture books by James Marshall and Harry Allard, which includes such titles as *The Stupids Have a Ball*, *The Stupids Step Out*, and *The Stupids Die*. Mr. and Mrs. Stupid are good role models for Mr. and Ms. Poetryhead.

In their upside-down world, only the normal is abnormal. They sleep with their feet on their pillows, they shower with their clothes on, they proudly do everything in exactly the wrong way. In *The Stupids Take Off*, the family visits various relatives, including cousin Patty Stupid. At Patty's birthday party, Buster, the son, has a precisely illogical exchange with her.

"Why are there eight candles on the cake?" asked Buster.

"Because I didn't have six," said Patty.

On several occasions, people have tried to censor the Stupids from schools and libraries. In Iowa City, the parents of a first grade girl were outraged at the use of *The Stupids Have a Ball*. In the book, Buster flunks all his classes, and the rest of the family throws a party for him. The first grader's parents took the book seriously enough to demand that it be withdrawn from the school system. When the school held a meeting to discuss the book, other families came to protest the attempt at censorship, and the book was left on the shelves.

It's difficult to imagine anyone thinking that the Stupids represent the way things should be. Even young children laugh at the craziness. They get a chance to see the world as it isn't, can't be, or shouldn't be.

CHAPTER 2

PHYSICAL POETRY— OTHER OBJECTS

"The time has come," the Walrus said,
"To talk of many things."

—Lewis Carroll, "The Walrus and the Carpenter"

26. POETRY LAMP

The light of inspiration literally shines through the Poetry Lamp. Its lampshade has poems written on it. To view them properly, flick the switch.

When I used this method with the Poetry Class for People over Sixty, I suggested they take turns writing directly on the lampshade, but they insisted on doing their first versions on paper so the final version on the shade would be without errors. One student, Benita Allen, who was also an artist, suggested that everyone include a sketch next to their poem. When they finished writing and drawing on the lamp, I turned it on. A warm orangish glow emanated through the words.

Description
The students write poems on paper and copy them onto a lampshade. When they're done, turn off the overhead light and turn on the lamp. Ask the students to come up to the lamp one at a time and read their poems.

Materials
lamp
lampshade (made of white or light translucent material)
lightbulb
black felt-tip pens
writing paper

Suggested Topics
1) "Light and dark—which do you prefer? Why is light important? Why is dark important?"
2) "What if the sky were so cloudy over the city that the sun couldn't be seen? How would this affect things?"

The students draw pictures next to their poems on the lampshade.

Examples

Without light
We have no color
Without color
Nature has lost
Her finery.

    —Benita Allen, PCPO-Sixty

The light of day
And the dark of night
Blend them together
What an inspiration
For a man-made lamp

    —Fanny Blair, PCPO-Sixty

The lamp on the sill
Of the old cabin window
Beckoned all who traveled
By horseback or foot.
So this lamp
On the tall brown spindle
Should guide all who
Study by its light.

    —Nellie Voelckers, PCPO-Sixty

27. HAND FAN WRITING

It was a hot day at the Senior Center. The students in the Poetry Class for People over Sixty finished writing poems on hand fans and put them to practical use. They fanned themselves in the cool breeze of poetry.

Advanced readers of poetry might want to heat their brains up by reading Stéphane Mallarmé's poems "A Fan" and "Another Fan."

Description
The students write poems on hand fans. They can take two different approaches: their lines can go in rainbow-like arcs horizontally across the fans, or they can branch upward and outward vertically along the folds.

Materials
paper hand fans
black felt-tip pens

Suggested Topics
1) "The wind can affect people in different ways. What are some good ways? What are some not so good ways?"
2) "Suppose the wind were a person taking things that belong to other people. What things does it take? Why does it take them? Where does it go with them?"
3) "Imagine that the fan is the wing of a bird. What does the bird look like? Where does it live? Is it tame or wild? How did you get its wing?"
4) "Hand fans have one main use—to cool people off. What other uses can you come up with? Write about a use that seems practical. Or one that seems totally off the wall."

Examples

> The wind shimmers thru the
>   trees at night
> The wind makes the trees bud
>   and the flowers to grow
> The wind comes from the
>   Majesty on High
> The wind helps the windmill go round
> God uses the wind for the crops to come
> Dear wind we need you in the summer
>
> —*Clarice Stenby, PCPO-Sixty*

Her majesty awaits within
Oh Master—come soon—
Slowly & gently blow about
Now

—*Fanny Blair, PCPO-Sixty*

28. POETRY CHAIR

The Poetry Chair is a beautiful and functional poetry object that money can't buy. When the whole class has covered it with poems, it takes on a meaning beyond words. It would make a good gift for a fellow teacher who is retiring or moving away.

Students in the Poetry Class for People over Sixty made the first Poetry Chair. Everyone loved the final product, and I looked forward to taking it home with me. However, Myldred Strong, one of the quieter students, asked if she could have it. I helped her carry it to her apartment.

A few weeks later, Myldred invited the class to meet at her place. There was the chair, standing in her living room just inside the entryway. She had varnished it to protect the wood and the poems.

Several years after I stopped teaching the class, I decided to contact Myldred. The people at the senior center told me she'd moved to a nursing home. The only piece of furniture she took with her was the Poetry Chair.

Description
The students write poems in regular stanzas on paper and copy them onto a wooden chair, or they write directly on the chair in lines that go every which way. (See the "Wooden Poetry Sculpture" method for another activity based on this approach.)

Materials
unfinished wooden chair
black felt-tip pens

Suggested Topics
1) "This is a chair that puts you in a certain mood when you sit down. Imagine sitting on it. How do you feel? Why do you feel that way?"
2) "Where did the chair come from? Who made it? Where did the wood come from? What was the forest like?"
3) "What kind of chairs are there?" (Possibilities include kitchen chair, wheelchair, throne, and electric chair.) "Pick one kind, and write about it on this chair."

Alternative

The students write poems on two chairs and a table. The resulting poetry objects can be displayed in the classroom reading area, the library, or the media center.

Examples

Happiness is dropping into a chair
When you are weary.
A chair that fits your body
And your mood.
Even if you are all alone
Relaxing in a chair
Makes you feel good,
Relaxes and gives you
Thought for food.

  —Alice Gratke, PCPO-Sixty

Patience

I sat many days in a small space
Almost hidden in this large storeroom
Customers came one after another
They looked at me, criticizing my looks
None were satisfied
One day a poet came looking
He saw my slim curving lines

And pictured in his mind
How I might sometimes look
I satisfied him. I am happy now I had to wait
And was patient.

—Nellie Voelckers, PCPO-Sixty

I am the Chair of Frustration
Sit back on me Pop goes my middle
So high you cannot see. Put your arm on my arm
I'll vibrate up and down. Put your hand on the alarm
And I give a squeaking sound

—Florence Walton, PCPO-Sixty

The Chair of Hope

Hope rises
    eternal
as one sits
    at the end
        of the day.
Hoping that
    tomorrow
Will be better
    than today

—Myldred Strong, PCPO-Sixty

29. WOODWORKS

Paper is just thin wood, as a student once said. Instead of writing on paper, try a sheet of wood. Though the two are similar, composing on wood is much different than composing on paper. The wood grain makes it bumpy. The ink bleeds into it, fuzzing and rippling across the surface. The side of your hand touching it as you write may rub over rough areas. It has the feel of old doors—one of the suggested topics of this writing.

I like to use wood that has a good smell. It's a great way to start off the writing. The first thing most students naturally do is smell the wood. Then they rub it in their hands, knock on it, or try to balance it on one edge.

Description
The students write on rectangular pieces of wood. To emphasize the difference from writing on paper, ask the students to rub their hands on a

sheet of paper and to smell it. Then hand out the wood and ask them to do the same with it.

Materials
rectangular pieces of wood of different sizes (1' or less on any side) colored felt-tip pens

Suggested Topics
1) "If the wood could talk, what would it tell you about the tree it came from? What kind of tree was it? How old was it?"
2) "The piece of wood is a small door. When you open it, you can enter a world where objects talk. What do you meet? What does it say?"

Alternative
The students write on both sides of irregularly shaped pieces of wood. On one side: "What was the original board's use?" On the other side: "What could you make out of this piece?"

Examples
The students from Southdale School in Cedar Falls were in fourth, fifth, and sixth grade. Their poems appeared in *Magic Hamburgers*, a classroom anthology.

When the Woods Were Young

When the woods were young and living
The birds were cheerful and singing
The deer had fun, the buffalo would run
When all the woods were living
When all the woods were dying
The men were strong and building
When all the men were done
The woods were dead and lying

—*Irene Sommer*

The Fine Wood

One day there was a little tree
    that truly adored me.
I went straight home
    so the tree was alone.

Then ten years went by
And the little tree cried
    for I had not been visiting him.
Another day went by
    and a ranger came by.
He said, "I am truly sorry

for your friend named Scary,
but it is time."

So he chopped up Scary
and I felt sorry.
He said he would use
his sledge hammer.
So he did,
and used Scary for insulation,
in his house.

—*Lisa Niedert*

Said the Kleenex
To the nose,
"To you, I propose
you are blowing
me to a shred;
You really should take to bed."
"NONSENSE!"
said the nasal drip.
"It's you that should
take a dip."
"Foo!" said the Puff so clear.
"You smell a lot like beer."
"HA!" said the owner of the nose.
"I'm full of woes and woes.
You guys shouldn't talk, it's the
ATCHOOO!"

—*Stephanie Carlson*

Once upon a time I went to Egypt.
I was there to study an old town.
While in the desert, one of my
camera legs sunk into the sand
in what?
Not rock! So I started to dig
and came to a room filled with
gold and stones. I found a
door, opened it and found a
mummy's coffin. I opened it,
unwrapped it and found
Queen Tonto.

—*Tom Morgan*

Clock Time

At certain times of the day certain
things talk.
And at certain times of the day
certain things walk.

6:00

For instance, a garbage can may say
"How dare you put your garbage in
me today," and then walk away.

7:00

And an encyclopedia may say: "I
know more than you," to a dummy.
And the dummy will walk away.

8:00

A door may say: "Don't knock me,
I'll hit you with my knob"
to a coat and the coat will walk away.

9:00

The doll will say: "Time to go to
sleep." And all the toys, dolls,
pencils, books, doors, clocks, and
garbage cans will all go to sleep.

10:00

The doll will say: "Up and at 'em."
All the things will get up and
start talking again.

   —*Becky Price*

A Screw

I am a screw inside a
big piece of wood all
I do is sit here and
do nothing, one day a
man just put me here
and just left me here
I've been here for about
three years.

   —*Kristen Spande*

A Piece of Wood

There's a story that has to be told,
About a piece of wood with one side old.
I think it should be read instead of sung,

About a piece of wood with one side young.
Both sides are on the same piece of wood.
People say it can't happen, but I think it could,
To keep your youth and never let go,
Don't let it leave like melting snow.

  —Elaine Wahrer

Later on, the older people wrote on irregularly shaped pieces of wood using the Alternative.

Well-Built

Certain people are called "square"—How nice to have the dimension of this small piece of wood

  —Pearl Minor, PCPO-Sixty

The Pine Tree

The Pine Tree grew
in a deep forest.
The lumbermen
felled it and stripped
off its branches.
It floated down a
stream with many
other pine logs.
At the mill the
saws cut it into
long strips that
soon became 2 by 4's.
When the builder
bought these 2 by 4's,

(On the other side)

this damaged section
was zipped off alas.
But the texture,
fragrance, and grain
of this beautiful
pine wood remain
the same to the
last inch. At a
fairy's touch it
could become
the figurine of

a fawn, the Pine
Tree's early friend,
and an ornament
of a Christmas tree.

—*Cora Pollock, PCPO-Sixty*

Siding

This piece of siding could've been the side of a bird house
But I got the windows in the wrong place
So this will probably slide right on to some man's desk
To help him think what to do next.
When he sees the two brown spots
He will remember that his two brown eyes
Really do need rest. Pleasant dreaming.

—*Alice Gratke, PCPO-Sixty*

30. WOODEN POETRY SCULPTURE

Lines of poetry follow the crisscrossing pieces of a wooden sculpture. The sculpture doesn't represent anything until poetry gives it meaning, and then it gives meaning to the poetry. The students create a collection of poetry objects ready for play or display.

The students in the Poetry Class for People over Sixty responded very differently to this activity than they did to the Poetry Chair activity discussed earlier. They didn't think about writing on paper first and then rewriting. Instead, their pens jumped right into the sculpture. Its 3-D crazy-quilt structure seems to encourage improvisation.

Description
The students glue eight to twelve pieces of wood to a square wooden base without trying to make it resemble anything. When the glue is dry, they write poems that zigzag around the surfaces of the wood and slide from one piece to the other.

Materials
irregularly shaped pieces of wood (20" or fewer in length)
quick-drying glue or wood glue
colored felt-tip pens

Suggested Topics
1) "You find this object in front of your home. What is it? Who left it there? Why? What will you do with it?"

Photo: Dom Franco

2) "This is a city of the future. What will you find in it? What would you want to see? How do people travel in it? Where do they live, work, shop, and play?"

3) "It's an artificial satellite orbiting the earth or shooting into outer space. What does it do? How far will it travel? Who shot it up there?"

Alternative

Make a single large wooden sculpture (four feet at its widest part) for the reading area and tell the students they can write on it in their free time. Challenge them to completely cover every piece of it with poetry during the school year.

31. CHOPSTICK QUATRAINS

Some chopsticks are made with four flat sides. Each student writes one line of poetry on each side, creating a quatrain. When everyone is finished, two or more students place their chopsticks together and rearrange them to make a collaborative poem.

Some students may want to write extra poems, so bring a generous supply of chopsticks to satisfy their hunger for literature. When I first tried this, at a congregate meals site, a couple of the students literally ate lunch with their poems.

Description
The students write four-line poems on flat-sided chopsticks, one line per side. Then they place the chopsticks together, rolling them over to make collaborative poems.

Materials
chopsticks
black felt-tip pens

Suggested Topics
1) "What is your favorite food? Why do you like it so much?"
2) "You try to eat alphabet soup with chopsticks, but you can pick up only one letter at a time. What would the soup spell?"

Alternative
Each student writes on two chopsticks, with all eight lines having the same rhythm and rhyme. (Students may need a rhyming dictionary.) When the finished chopsticks are placed next to each other, every combination of two sides forms a rhyming couplet.

Examples

Red & juicy
Eat with or without another delicacy
Put seasoning, sauce, or whatever
The tomato—king of all, ruler of the garden.
　　—Fanny Blair, PCPO-Sixty

A bowl of fat red berries
Topped with luscious cream
Healthful raspberries from my garden
My favorite gourmet dream.
　　—Benita Allen, PCPO-Sixty

How will I eat Chinese tea?
Chop Sticks, Chop Sticks, will you master me?
I like cherry pie
Don't give me honey
　　—Myldred Strong, PCPO-Sixty

32. BOWL POEM

If you wrote on a wooden bowl, where would you start writing? What shape would your lines take? Think about that for a minute, and then read on.

When I first used this activity, I asked the students (nine elementary school teachers) to take turns writing a single poem on the bowl, but I didn't specify the pattern of the words or the writing area. They formed the poem in a spiral down the inside surface.

This showed me again something that, although it should be obvious, still surprises me: the shapes of things strongly influence the shapes of writing. Poetry usually appears in rectangular form when it's written on rectangular sheets of paper. If you use a different shape of paper, you'll probably write a different shape of poem.

What shape would your writing follow? What shape would your students' words take?

Description

The students each write a poem on a wooden bowl using colored pens. Before the writing, they can discuss where to write the words—outside or inside the bowl, center to edge or edge to center, one line or many lines, etc.

Materials

wooden salad bowls (6" to 8" in diameter)
colored felt-tip pens

Suggested Topics

1) "A crumb is lying at the bottom of the bowl. Write a poem from the point of view of a line of ants marching down to get it. What food is the crumb? How did the ants find out about it?"
2) "There's magic cereal in the bowl. When you eat it, it gives you one magic power. What is it? How would you use it?"
3) "What could you put in this bowl instead of food?"

33. POETRY WOODEN NICKELS

Wooden nickels are great for short poems! Students love writing on them, and afterwards they can carry them around in their pockets. You may not have known that wooden nickels exist. Most people don't, except for hearing "Don't take any wooden nickels." But there are billions of them! They're the size of silver dollars with an American Indian or a buffalo pictured on one side and a message printed on the other. The surface is just the right size and shape for a quick drawing or poem.

I've used them with students and with people of all ages. When I show the wooden nickels to the students, their first response is to smile, and then they want to try doing one of their own.

One teacher asked her students to draw on the nickels but to write on paper, to allow for a longer poem. Her students took the wooden nickels and got creative!

Description
Everyone writes and/or draws on a wooden nickel, and then draws and/or writes on a sheet of paper. There should be a lot of room for personal interpretation in this activity.

Materials
wooden nickels
drawing paper
colored felt-tip pens (and any other art materials you want)

Preparation
The wooden nickels have to be ordered from a wooden nickel company. You specify what is to be printed on them. Recommended copy: PO-ETRY WOODEN NICKEL around the rim, and perhaps your name, grade, and school in the center. Specify that you want the other side to be left blank, or the manufacturer will probably print an image of an American Indian or a buffalo on it.

Where to order? Only eight or ten companies print wooden nickels. The biggest and oldest is the Elbee Co., whose colorful owner, Leonard Berkie, has become a living legend as the wooden nickel magnate of the world. The nickels are cheap—250 for about $30—and well worth the price. For more information, send $2.35 for twenty-five different sample nickels and a current catalogue to:

Elbee Co.
520 Broadway, Box 230-CW
San Antonio, TX 78291
(210) 223-4561

Suggested Topics
1) "Think about some object you really like—something you own or would like to own. Or some person you really like—a friend, a movie star, an athlete, a cartoon character. Using a piece of paper and a wooden nickel, write your thoughts on one, and a draw a picture on the other."
2) "What is your own personal motto? Write that on the nickel, and then draw a picture on paper to go with it."

3) "Look for ideas in the wood grain. What does it remind you of? What shapes are in it?"

Each student gets two nickels. He or she writes on one and draws on the other.

Examples

My Dogs

My dogs are very special.

One of my dogs was given to me
on my birthday.

One was born from the one
I got for my birthday.

We're going to give my baby dog away.

Some day.

> —*Malynda McCure, fourth grade*

The Butterfly

The butterfly is so shy
It hides from many things
It can go high in the world
But when it dies,
It flutters softly to the ground

> —*Jana Brooke Davidson, fourth grade*

> This is a shattered
windshield of a car
> going down the highway

> —*Jon Kimmel, fourth grade*

My Whale

There she goes
said my friend
There she blows
said I

> —*Nathan Druivenga, fourth grade*

34. POETRY PAINTING

Writing and painting blend together to make lively poetry objects. This activity is similar to children's drawings, which naturally combine words and pictures. It is a basic mixture of two media, and it's one of the most popular with students of all ages.

Faced with a canvasboard, one or two students may express reluctance. "I don't know how to paint," some might say. The teacher explains that they aren't really painting, because they won't use a brush. Instead, they use a pen with its cap on to swirl the paint around without trying to represent anything. This dispels any fears about making realistic images, and they will have no objections to using the word *painting* for the activity.

Students' poetry paintings usually turn out to be visually and verbally imaginative—ideal for an exhibit.

Description

The teacher puts three dabs of color (red, blue, and yellow) on each student's board. Using either end of a capped felt-tip pen as a brush, the student paints an abstract image on one half of a canvasboard. Then he or she removes the cap and writes a poem about the image on the other half.

Materials

small canvasboards (5" x 7" or so)
acrylic paint (red, blue, and yellow)
black felt-tip pens

Suggested Topics

1) "What do you see in your painting? Are there any people, animals, objects? What feelings do the shapes and colors represent?"
2) "Paint speaks its own language. What is it saying in your picture?"

Alternatives

1) Each student paints with pen on canvas, leaving an open space for words. Then everyone swaps canvases and writes on someone else's canvas.
2) Same procedure as the previous alternative, but the students write first, then trade and paint.
3) Several students write and paint a collaboration on a larger canvasboard or stretched canvas (24" x 36" or larger).

The Sun Shining Through

The sun shining through
A rose
To make the earth more
Beautiful

—*Gladys Edwards, PCPO-Sixty*

One huge lone tree
In the African jungle
Stands guard over all.

—*Nellie Voelckers, PCPO-Sixty*

A kid with
   the measles

Or perhaps only
   bright new
      freckles

On a hot
   afternoon

—*Edna Gingerich, PCPO-Sixty*

35. FACE-PAINTING POEMS

Painting on faces is often part of school festivals and other celebrations. At the next festival, try putting poetry on the faces. The participants become walking, talking poems, which raises W. B. Yeats's question, "How can you tell the dancer from the dance?"

Description

Three or four students manage a poetry face-painting table at a school festival. They ask each customer for a topic, and then they make up a one-line or one-word poem on the spot (see "Minimal Poetry" below). If the customer likes it, one student paints it, along with other designs, on the customer's face

Materials

black felt-tip pens
writing paper
wide, colored felt-tip pens
posterboard

table
4–5 chairs
clown face paint
2–3 eyebrow pencils

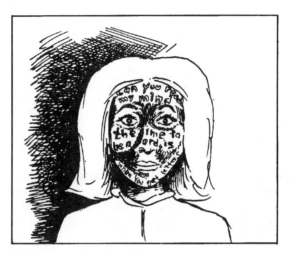

Preparation

You and your assistants set up the table, chairs, sign, face paint, and eyebrow pencils. Then you're in business. Copy the poems on paper to read later in class, and photograph the faces that turned out especially well.

Suggested Topics

1) "Do you have anything you'd like to say about the festival?"
2) "How about making up a two-line poem about school?"
3) "Do you have any pets you'd like to write about?"
4) "Any hobbies?"
5) "What's your favorite sport? Do you like watching it or playing it or both?"
6) "Do you like music? What kind? Do you play an instrument?"
7) "Do you like to read? What kind of books?"
8) "What do you want to be when you get older? Why?"
9) "Have you ever been to a foreign country? What did you like most about it?"
10) "How about a poem for your boyfriend (girlfriend, husband, wife, son, daughter)?"

•

Minimal Poetry

Since the 1960s, some poets have written what might be called minimal poetry. In visual art, *minimal* is associated with conceptual art. In poetry, it often applies to poems with very few words.

Minimal poetry hasn't gotten maximum acceptance. It appears now and then in literary magazines, but it no longer has the following it once had. Perhaps its minimalness keeps it on the boundaries of poetry. In any event, minimal poetry can be—in a word—fun.

In the 1960s, Aram Saroyan spent several years writing poetry that got shorter and shorter. His first minimal works were two or more lines long, containing a total of six to eight words—for instance, "crickets" written eight times in a column. Then he decided a single line was enough, and he composed a few one-line poems. Next he wrote one-word poems, such as "Blod" and "lighght." The latter, a wonderfully mysterious variation on its dictionary counterpart, won an $800 literary award, which may represent the most money a single poem has ever earned in a day—$134.28 per letter.

In the 1970s, one-word poetry had its own magazine, *Matchbook*, edited by Joyce Holland. *Matchbook*'s one-square-inch pages were stapled inside real matchbooks. Each issue showcased nine words, one per page, with the poet's name on the facing page. Eleven examples from *Matchbook* show the variety of possible approaches to a one-word poem:

razzmatazz (Paul Violi)
john (John Sjoberg)
acetylcholinesterase (John Batki)
lups (Michael Lally)
sixamtoninepm (Kit Robinson)
groblems (Edwin Denby)
underwhere (Carol DeLugach)
electrolocution (Scott Wright)
injest (Audrey Teeter)
puppylust (P. J. Casteel)
embooshed (Cinda Kornblum)

If your initial response is, "My kids could do that," well, you're absolutely right. And they would have fun in the process.

36. BANANAVERSE

Bananas, according to one commercial, are nature's perfect food. The smooth peel also makes a perfect surface for writing a poem that goes bananas.

Description
Each student writes a poem on a banana, reads it, peels it, and eats it. (Eating the banana is optional.)

Materials
bananas
black felt-tip pens (non-toxic ink)

Suggested Topic
"You have a choice: Tell the banana why it should be happy you're going to eat it, or have the banana tell you why it isn't happy you're going to eat it."

37. PEANUT POEMS

Fortune cookies have little messages printed on paper wrapped inside the crispy shells. Peanut poems are the opposite. They have little messages written directly on the outside of their shells. When someone cracks open the peanut, they crack the poem, too.

Description
The students write one-line poems on the shells of unopened peanuts (see "Minimal Poetry" in method 35). Put them in a bowl. Then have each student take out a peanut, read it aloud, and write down the poem on it. Then he or she eats the peanut. Afterwards, everyone writes a poem with the peanut shell line in it.

Materials
bowl of peanuts
black felt-tip pens (non-toxic ink)

Suggested Topics
1) "Write a one-sentence poem predicting a person's future. As with fortune cookie fortunes, the peanut predictions should be upbeat and cheery."
2) "Elephants are supposed to love to eat peanuts. Write about something elephants don't do with peanuts. You could begin, "Elephants don't. . . .""

1) Each student writes a poem on two or more peanuts. After everyone reads, cracks, and eats one peanut apiece, send the remaining peanut poems to another class. The other teacher distributes them to the students, who likewise read, crack, and eat them.

2) Two classes make peanut poems and trade bowls of peanuts.

38. POETRY CAKE

The idea of combining writing with cake comes from ancient Jewish tradition. Early in their history, the Jews baked honey cakes in the shape of letters for the children in order to show them that knowledge is sweet.

I've created poetry cakes for two weddings. The first couple divorced two years later. The second couple are still together and have four children. The second poem was much better than the first.

Description
The students take turns writing poetry on a cake. They squeeze icing from a cake-decorator's tube to spell out the words. When the poem is finished, everyone eats it.

Materials
cake with a single color of icing
bowl of a second icing (color should contrast with the cake's icing)
cake decorator's tube

1) "This will be a Poetry Cake. How would eating poetry be different than writing it? How would it be the same?"
2) "Words have flavors, and we need a vanilla word here. How about a chocolate word here. Watch out for stale words."
3) "Today the school is celebrating _____. Let's write about it."
4) "Now that winter's here, compare the (white) icing to a snowy scene."

Suggestions
1) Be aware that the smaller the words are printed, the less legible they will be.
2) Take photographs: that way you can have your cake and eat it, too.

Alternative
Instead of one large cake, use a tray of smaller cupcakes, enough for everybody to have one. To write the poem, each student squeezes one word on a cupcake.

39. BALL POEM

Writing on a ball is an obvious way to alter the writing process. There are many kinds of balls in different sizes, textures, and shapes that words can cover in many different ways. The method below starts the ball rolling.

Description
Each student writes a continuous line of poetry on a ball. The words can spiral around and down, or they can curve in different ways and cross over what has already been written.

Materials
balls (various sizes, from baseball to basketball)
black felt-tip pens

Suggested Topics
1) "Suppose the ball were going to be used in a sport. What sport would it be? What message would be on it?"
2) "Let's say it's a crystal ball. What predictions would it make about you?"
3) "Imagine you're about to take a cruise around the world. Where would you go? How would you travel? Who would go with you?"

4) "The ball is a tiny planet, and it's fallen to earth. Only one creature lives on it. What does that creature look like? What would you say to it, and how would it reply?"

40. BALLOON POEMS

Some balloon poems end with a bang! Others float away to be forever lost in the ozone. It's loud light verse. When I put pen to balloon at the Cedar Rapids Art Festival, I encountered a technical difficulty: in the sunlight, the pen's ink sometimes eats through the rubber, causing a balloon to pop. I found that this happens less in the shade.

Most of my collaborators were either young children and their parents, teenage girls (much more than teenage boys), or couples in love. A few asked for more than one balloon, and some came back later for seconds. The poems were short, humorous pieces. I simply took the words and ideas the festival-goers suggested and fashioned them into poems on the balloons. Given the choice between rhyme and free verse, most people picked rhyme.

But not every time.

Description
During a school festival, the teacher and three or four students set up a poetry booth. The festival-goers can make up short poems and write them on balloons, or they can suggest topics to the students, who do the writing for them. In either case, they get to keep the finished Poetry Balloons. (An option is to copy the poems into a notebook.)

Materials
wide, colored felt-tip pens
posterboard (for a sign)
table
4–5 chairs
tank of helium
balloons
scissors
string

Preparation
The teacher and student assistants set up everything, including table, chairs, sign, and helium tank. Then they inflate and tie up a few balloons.

Suggested Topics
For a list of possibilities, see Suggested Topics in the "Face-Painting Poems" method (activity 35).

Suggestion
Copy the poems on paper and read them to the students during the next class meeting.

Examples

Dog

A dog
On a log
Would bark
At bark.

Turtle

Although
He's slow,
His shell
Works well.

Friends

A friend is better
Than an Irish Setter
Or a schnauzer
Named "Bowser"
Or a collie
Named "Mollie."

A friend is human
Like Harry Truman.

—*Dave Morice and various collaborators*

41. FOAM RUBBER MOON

What would it be like to write on the moon? Its surface, pocked with craters, would create unusual challenges. Since most of us are stranded on earth for the time being, we have to find reasonable lunar substitutes.

The material for this exercise, large blocks of foam rubber, came from the Physics Department at the University of Iowa. I'd seen the blocks piled high in a hallway one night as a friend of mine and I were going up to the observatory. I immediately thought, "Such is the stuff that poetry is made of." The next day, after getting permission, I hauled ten of the foam rubber blocks to class.

Description
The students make a list of five words referring to the moon and five referring to the earth. Using these words and their own words to connect them, they write poems on blocks of foam rubber.

Materials
foam rubber blocks (roughly 6" x 6" x 18")
wide and thin black felt-tip pens
writing paper

Suggested Topics
1) "Imagine you've landed on the moon. You step down on the surface and discover it's spongy. You cut a piece out with your knife, take your laser pen out of your space suit, and start to write about what you see—the moon's surface, the earth, and the stars."
2) "The moon's gravity is only one-sixth of earth's. If you weigh 120 pounds on earth, you'd weigh only 20 pounds on the moon. You could jump much higher and farther. What would you do up there? How would the low gravity affect playing your favorite sport?"

Suggestions
1) Physical fitness gyms sometimes have pits filled with foam rubber blocks for kids to play in. You might request a donation of a bunch of blocks in exchange for acknowledging the gym on a sign when you display the Foam Rubber Poems.
2) To exhibit the blocks in the classroom, pile them up in the reading area. Students can use them as cushions.

Examples

In the first poem below, the author wrote the two stanzas on different sides of the block.

Downstairs

Downstairs
you look like a copper canoe on sky water.
When I saw you rise, Moon,
you looked like a pumpkin
grinning.
O, lend me your mountains, Moon!

You look like a marble
up here, Earth,
a great blue agate.
Down there rivers run
through green
from pole to pole.

—Pearl Minor, PCPO-Sixty

The man from the spacecraft
Was standing on the moon
He looked for rocks
Some were big, some round
The terrain was gray,
full of chemicals,
enough for a list to fill an 8 x 11 sheet

—Myldred Strong, PCPO-Sixty

42. ROCK POETRY

Writing on the irregular surface of rocks challenges the penmanship of the best of us, and that's part of the fun. This project can tie in with a discussion of Native American petroglyphs as well as rock writing and cave painting by other cultures.

On a car trip out west, I saw some modern rock writing in the Mojave Desert. Over the years, travelers have arranged rocks to form letters in the sand along the roadside. For miles and miles, the rocky letters spell out initials, names, and cryptic messages.

Description

The students write poems on rocks and arrange them in a shallow box to make a rock garden. They can add other materials (dirt, sand, leaves, branches) to build a more elaborate display.

Materials
colored felt-tip pens
rocks (about the size of baseballs)
shallow wooden or cardboard box
sand, dirt, leaves, etc.

Suggested Topics
1) "If the rock could speak, what would it tell you about its long life on earth?"
2) "Imagine you're a cave dweller, and you want to write a letter to a friend. The rock is your form of mail. What do you write?"
3) "As a cave dweller, you decide to leave an important message for the future. What is your message?"

Alternatives
1) Each student writes one word on twenty to thirty smaller rocks, arranges them in lines on a posterboard, and glues them in place.
2) The students arrange pebbles on the sidewalk to form letters that spell the words of their poems.

43. SAND SCRIPT

Sand is fascinating. Children spend hours playing in sandboxes, scooping the sand around, making shapes, and throwing it into the air. Maria Montessori even taught children to write by means of sand trays. Using their fingers, her students wrote the alphabet in the sand. And the Mojave Indians have been creating intricate full-color sand paintings for centuries.

In this poetry activity, sand is the page and fingers are the pencils.

Description
Using a finger, the student writes a poem in a tray of sand and copies it (with a pencil) onto paper. The next student smoothes the sand by hand and writes a new poem.

Materials
sand tray (36" x 24" x 3")
black felt-tip pens
writing paper

Preparation
Pour sand in the tray and smooth it around to form a uniform half-inch surface.

1) "Have you ever built a castle in the sand? What would it be like to live in one?"

2) "You're lost in a desert. Weak from thirst and heat, you climb to the top of a dune. On the other side, you see something incredible, but you're afraid it's a mirage. What is it?"

3) "Pretend you're at the beach on a hot day. What do you like best to do there? Why?"

Alternative
If your school is near a beach or a desert, arrange a class field trip so you can do this "on site" for more expansive poems.

44. CERAMIC POETRY

If you have access to a ceramics studio, your students can make wonderful poetry objects out of clay. The experience of manipulating the clay to form words is much different from that of writing with pencil or pen. And when the clay is fired, the poem is transmuted from one form to another by ceramic magic.

At a high school in Pennsylvania, I worked with students who wrote poems on paper taped to the walls of a Poetry Room. Toward the end of this activity, two students brought a tray with three clay shapes on them—two tablets and a face. They asked if I'd carve a poem into each, so I did. They left with the raw clay poems and later returned with brown ceramic poetry objects.

Description
Using a stylus and a baseball-sized hunk of clay, each student fashions a shape and carves a poem in it. The ceramicist glazes the finished clay objects and fires them in a kiln.

Materials
clay
stylus
glaze
kiln

Suggested Topics
1) "What object will you mold? What will you use it for?"

2) "What does writing on clay feel like? Can you compare it to anything else you've ever done? How is it different from paper?"

3) "Imagine you are a prehistoric cave dweller, and you've just invented writing. What would you write to convince everyone else that writing is so important?"

1) Write on ceramic cups, saucers, bowls, plates. Use colorful glazes to emphasize the words.
2) Make poetry pottery to sell at a craft fair. Ceramic poems add variety to the usual offerings of non-verbal pots and vases.

Example

Tablet Number 1

When the
mouth
sees its
voice,
the eye
writes
aloud.
  —Dave Morice

Artist George Schneeman and poet Ron Padgett collaborated on a ceramic jar, whose lid had the prefix *un-* written on it in such a way that when the lid was rotated, the *un-* matched up with four different words written down the side of the jar: *lucky, wanted, loved,* and *derwear.*

45. WINDOW POEMS

Writing on a window is a simple way to include the world in a poem. Concrete poet Ian Hamilton Finlay placed a poem on a pane of glass. The poem showed the word *wave* crashing into the word *rock*, but the background varies, depending on where the reader holds the glass.

Artist Marcel Duchamp used a window in his monumentally complex "Large Glass." Legend has it that after the work was returned from an exhibition, Duchamp opened the carton only to find hundreds of cracks in the glass. He looked at the worried shippers and said, "Now it's complete!"

Like the works of Finlay and Duchamp, this activity has a transparent twist to it: the second stanza drastically changes the way that both stanzas would normally look.

Description
The students write poems in one color on the inside of a window. A week later, they write poems in a different color on the outside. They arrange both poems back-to-back.

scissors
cloth or paper towels (for wiping off mistakes)
windows (accessible from both sides)
fabric markers (colored)

Suggested Topics
1) *For all windows:*
First half: "What do you see through the window? What is the biggest thing? The smallest? Are any people on the other side? What are they doing?" Second half: "Now what do you see? How is it different from what you saw through the first side? How do the words on the window affect what you see?"
2) *For windows with a view outside:*
First half: "How does it feel to be inside? What would you do if you were outside?" Second half: "How does it feel to be outside? What would you do if you were inside?"

Suggestion
Through the window, take photographs of students looking at their poems.

Alternatives
1) One student writes the first half on one side. A week later, another student writes the second half on the other side. The second half replies to the first half.
2) Two students write on opposite sides at the same time.

46. MIRROR VERSE

Mirrors fascinate both children and adults. Lewis Carroll knew this, and he showed Alice the way to the Looking-Glass World. When students write on mirrors, they touch a reality that is both familiar and strange. They watch themselves writing about themselves.

Some students may feel self-conscious at first, but once the words start coming, they enjoy this unusual experience. After the writing, they can experience poetry in an entirely different way. Two students hold their mirrors facing each other, and the poems on them recede in an infinity of images. Each can read the other's poem correctly, but his or her own shows up backwards. To orient the poems so the writers can read their own, they exchange mirrors and then view them.

Students may enjoy Guillaume Apollinaire's poem written in the shape of an oval mirror (in his book *Calligrams*, translated by Anne Hyde Greet and published by the University of California Press).

Description

The students write small "songs of myself" with different colored fabric markers on hand mirrors while reflecting on their own reflections. You might have them read Whitman's "Song of Myself" first.

Materials

hand mirrors
colored fabric markers
scissors
cloth or paper towels

Suggested Topics

1) "What do you see when you look in the mirror?"
2) "If the face in the mirror could tell you something about yourself, what would it tell you?"
3) "If you could ask your mirror image something, what would you ask? How would your image reply?"

Alternative

Using one full-length mirror, each student in a small group writes a poem whose lines twist, turn, and cross over the other students' poems. Each uses a different colored fabric marker.

Examples

> Look into the mirror
> face to face
> Will it be wonderful
> or a disgrace
> If you do not like it
> start to do something about
> it   Look again & see if
>   it please thee
>   if it does, Well done
>
>   —*Gladys Edwards, PCPO-Sixty*

> This is the moment
>   of truth
> For you cannot hide
> My imperfections
> But when I am happy
> It is good of you
> To reflect the sparkle
> In my eyes
>
>   —*Benita Allen, PCPO-Sixty*

I smile back at
myself
to convince *me*.

—Pearl Minor, PCPO-Sixty

47. STYROFOAM HEADS

Some people claim to be mind-readers. They say they can "hear" the
unspoken thoughts. In this activity, the students become "mind-writers,"
making poems on the craniums of styrofoam heads.

Since the writing involves heads, it can be preceded by discussion
of many intriguing topics that aren't usually discussed in school, such
as the fact that the brain operates at only five percent of capacity. Split-
brain theory says that we do math with the right side and make art with
the left. Criminologists used to believe you could tell whether a person
had a criminal mind by the shape of the head. Fortune-tellers read palms
to tell a person's future, but phrenologists read head-bumps. We live
two lives—our waking life and our dream life.

The students make a different kind of poetry on each of two heads,
and then a third kind on paper. These parallel creations involve students
in alternative ways of manipulating words.

Description
The students glue cut-out magazine words to make a collage poem on
one head, and they write a collaborative poem in different colors of ink
on the other head. Then they write individual poems in black ink on
paper.

Materials
scissors
magazines
styrofoam heads (available through some large department stores, cloth-
    ing shops, and fabric shops)
colored felt-tip pens
black felt-tip pens
writing paper

Preparation
Cut out words from magazine article titles.

Suggested Topics
1) "The two heads are having a conversation. The first head speaks the
words that are taped on it. The second head replies—saying what? Together, write a reply on its head, and then write your own poem on paper."

2) "The phrases on the first head are its thoughts, and the second head can read the first head's mind. What does the second head think about what it sees? Write a collaborative reply on the head and your own poem on paper."

Example

[FIRST HEAD—COLLAGE LINES]

COAST ON luck   Rent FARM building
*
ONLY bucks and gasoline runs Everywhere
*
listening more than play When you have eyes to VIEW
*
one should KEEP beautiful tomorrows
*
Forever look TO this GOD
*
HOW'RE YOU
*
international mileage charge
*
there's unleaded whiskey
*
listen you've been educational
Free book
SPEAK
in Every World
*
we in flying your gold wins anywhere
only one car stopped couple

[SECOND HEAD—HANDWRITTEN LINES]

The world in this head
is fashioning the world of tomorrow,
feeding the hungry of the world,
Peace Corps
*
Greed will
overpower
the universe.
Wake up
everyone!
*

We love each other with our minds
    and hearts
*

Christ in all
    our hearts
*

THE EYE SEES YOU

*—Fanny Blair, Gladys Edwards, Clarice Stenby, Myldred Strong,
and Dave Morice, PCPO-Sixty*

48. POETRY SHIRT

White shirts covered with letters combine fashion design and poetry. When I first tried this, I was surprised at how nice the poemized shirt looked. But the ink was not quite waterproof, and the poetry eventually faded away in the wash.

The teachers in my Alternative Poetry Writing Methods class at the University of Iowa suggested that the Poetry Shirt would make a good gift for a teacher who was moving away or retiring.

Students might be interested to learn that as far back as the First World War, artist Sonia Delaunay was creating clothing with words written on it.

Description
The students write on a white shirt. For legibility, the poems probably shouldn't stray too far from stanzaic form. Make sure that the students are writing on the outside of the shirt and not on the inside.

Materials
white dress shirts (or T-shirts)
colored felt-tip pens

Preparation
Have students bring in a new or old white dress shirt (or T-shirt).

Suggested Topics
1) "Write a poem about a part of the body. I'll give each of you a different part." (Name one part for each student.)
2) "This shirt gives a superhuman power to the person wearing it. What is that power? How can it be used?"
3) "We're going to give a Poetry Shirt to [teacher's name]. How will the different parts of the shirt remind [him or her] of the school? What will the pocket remind [him or her] of? How about the sleeves? The cuffs? Let's fill it up with good memories and wishes."

After each student has made a Poetry Shirt, he or she passes it to the person on the right and receives a shirt from the person on the left. Then everyone writes another poem. This continues until every student in the group has written a poem on every shirt. The students keep their own shirts. (This works best with a small group.)

Examples

Look
  up, the sun
    is slowly
     becoming
    obscure

    —Fanny Blair, PCPO-Sixty

Arms have charms
Some are comely
Others help the lover
But yours draw the glances
Of the accomplished dancers.

    —Cora Pollock, PCPO-Sixty

Blessed are the feet
that carry good tidings
for they shall wear
their shoes in Heaven
      *

Poetry binds
   the hearts
Like cuffs bind
   the wrist
      *

It takes a backbone
  or a spine
To write a poem
  or print a line
      *

How would
we write
  without
     muscles?

Try it.
      *

Roll up the sleeves
when the writing gets
Tough.

—Gladys Edwards, PCPO-Sixty

CHAPTER 3

ENVIRONMENTAL POETRY

In the world of words, the imagination is one of the forces of nature.
—Wallace Stevens, "Adagia"

ONE WAY to dramatize the writing process is to alter the environment of the writing area. When the environment plays a larger than usual role, the act of writing becomes, at least in part, an act of theater. There's more action going on. The students might have to hop over words, crouch down to write, or duck to avoid a poem suspended from twine. If students from other classes ask what's going on, they become part of the drama.

When the writing takes place in the community, the passersby become part of the process, too. They might ask questions, offer words, or suggest ideas. Even the most innocent bystander can become a subject of the poem, an actor in the drama of writing. As Shakespeare said, "All the world's a stage."

Most of the activities in the chapter are grouped by the way in which paper is used to change the writing environment—by wrapping around it, hanging in it, floating in it, or shaping it. The last three methods, however, distort the environment by affecting the writer's senses.

After the writing activity, the students remove the paper and clean up the writing area, like stagehands removing scenery and props. The products are poems, but the process is what the students really remember. To preserve that memory, the teacher may want to photograph the work in progress.

In outdoor activities, the weather plays a significant role. If nature isn't cooperative, the poem may have to be postponed on account of rain.

49. POEM WRAPPING THE SCHOOL

What better way for students to end the week? Wrap up classes by wrapping the school in poetry. I've used this as the culminating activity for several five-day residencies in elementary schools. It allows for greater mobility than most of the activities. After all, there's so much space for standing and writing and socializing. The poems are up on the wall for

everyone to see, but none of my students has ever acted intimidated by the publicity of it all.

During the writing, there's always a lot of gossip, laughter, and fun. The students walk around and look at what their friends are doing. They joke about a line or an image. They peek over other students' shoulders. They talk about poetry in the same way they talk about their other interests, and it becomes more a part of their day, not something strange and remote.

Since this activity takes place outside, the weather influences the writing, sometimes in drastic ways. At one school, a strong prairie wind whisked a ten-foot long piece of paper off the wall and blew it across the playground. The students retrieved it from the fence where it lay trapped. Maybe I should have brought in Shelley's "Ode to the West Wind."

If you want to see how quickly students can become poets, say to them, "Today we're going to wrap the school in poetry."

Description

The students write poems (and draw pictures if they want) on a long sheet of paper taped all the way around the outside of the school building. They also collaborate on a single poem by telling words and ideas to the teacher, who writes it in one long line around the school. Several classes participate at the same time or at intervals throughout the day. They should spend a single class period (or more) outside during the activity.

Materials

rolls of white paper (24" wide and long enough to go around the perimeter of the school building)
strapping tape
scissors
wide, colored felt-tip pens

Preparation

Five or six students tape the paper around the building, cutting it at entrances and exits. Local printing or paper companies may be able to donate leftover spools of paper for the activity; otherwise, adding machine tape and thin felt-tip pens will do.

Suggested Topics

1) "What do you see around you? What do you hear? Smell? Feel? What do you notice that you've never noticed before?"
2) "Which is your favorite room in school? Which your least favorite? Compare the two."

Suggestion

I've always taken dictation from the students, with the other teachers there to make sure everything went smoothly. Instead of having the teacher writing the words of the collaborative poem, try having the students write them.

Examples

In their original forms, each of these two poems went in a single line around the school building.

At the Corner, The Wall Turns
(Excerpt)

At the corner, the wall turns to the winter sky. Grey clouds drop their degrees on the banks of the Urbandale parking lot. Cars roll in the cold street. The building's bricks shiver from the roof to the ground. My fingers are freezing to the words, but I'm wearing clothes to keep my cool. Where are the heaters? Who's hiding the sunshine? You need more light today for the weather writes a chilly surprise. Our plants are hiding. (They fear snow.) The girl whistles to the lost dog, whose tail wags in the shadow of the school. Our morning paper tells us the news, and the weird TV repeats it at night. . . .

—*Dave Morice and junior high school students*

Writing in the Rain

At the start of a gray day, the wet minutes orbit the Milky Way. We're marking all over the walls of this planet. Now they spell the words of the world. Like UFO's, the ABC's light up the paper sky. Do you believe in flying syllables? They cross the horizon before you can say "Take your time!" The rain increases: the water creases the page. Thirsty? Just open your mouth and say "AHHH!" Let your tongue be your umbrella. Each drop is a letter in a cloudy poem about the future of spring. How do you write to A or B without mentioning C? It ain't easy today! The small germs of light drift into your teeth, those tiny lightbulbs screwed into the roof (and the floor) of your mouth. Maybe now you can see what you're saying.

—*Dave Morice and fifth and sixth grade students*

50. POETRY PATH IN THE SCHOOLYARD

When I taught in Ankeny, Iowa, a fourth grade teacher suggested painting a poem on the playground. We asked the principal, and he was all for the idea. On the fifth and final day of my visit, the students and I created a permanent Poetry Path.

Since I was a visitor at their school, I merely facilitated the writing of the poem. (I painted it, which is what they really wanted to do.) One student would yell a word, and the others would respond with cheers or silence, depending on whether or not they liked it. As the poem grew longer and the paint dried, some of the students amused themselves by jumping from letter to letter.

About fifteen years later, the undergraduate students in my Children's Literature class introduced themselves by saying their names, their hometowns, and their interests. One student said she was from Ankeny. I asked her if she knew about the Poetry Path at the elementary school. "Yes, that's where I went to school," she said. "It's still there." Immortal verse.

Description
The students suggest words and phrases that might be used, and the teacher paints the poem in two- to three-foot tall letters around the outer limits of the schoolyard. Depending on the poem's length, the activity lasts from two to four hours. Several classes can take turns working on it.

Materials
yellow highway paint
6" paintbrush
concrete or blacktop surface in the schoolyard

Suggested Topic
"Where is this path going? What do you want to tell kids in the future about this poem? What can they do with it? What do you want to say about the school?"

Suggestion
Photograph everyone working on the Poetry Path. In the coming years, new students might be curious to know who made it.

Alternative
Each student writes a four- to eight-line poem in class and goes outside to paint it in small letters on the playground. Each poem occupies a ten- to fifteen-inch square space and functions as a stepping-stone for poetic feet.

Example

Poetry Path
[written in a single line]

Follow the yellow poetry path across the blacktop,
step on all the letters, and ride the alphabet train
till you reach the end of the line!

—Dave Morice and fourth–sixth grade students

51. POEM WHITEWASHED ON A STREET

This activity produces the largest poem in the book: some letters might wind up being fifteen feet tall. Because of that, the poem has just a few words, but it can be read from an airplane!

During the first and only Nonesuch Fair in Iowa City, I spent five or six hours writing a poem with a mop and whitewash on a downtown street that was blocked off to traffic. Rock and bluegrass music blasted from loudspeakers in the minipark at the corner. Jugglers, dancers, actors, magicians, and others performed on the street. Passersby came up to me and suggested words for the poem. As the verse grew, people walked along the words and rode their bicycles between the letters. Children played hopscotch on it.

The next day I got permission from two building owners to climb up to their roofs and take bird's-eye view photos. The whitewashed letters stayed readable for a couple of weeks. Then a heavy rainstorm erased them.

During a local art festival, teacher and students take turns whitewashing a poem on a closed-off city street. Anyone can suggest words and ideas for the poem. Since it is part of a festival, the writing continues throughout the day.

Materials
3–4 buckets of whitewash
mop (traditional type) or paint roller

Preparation
Arrange for the street to be blocked off during the festival. On the day of the writing, mix the whitewash and bring it with a mop to the site.

Alternative
If time, space, and circumstances permit, provide extra whitewash and mops for other participants to make smaller poems near the big one.

52. POEM WRAPPING A CITY BLOCK

Wrapping a city block in a poem makes poetry a part of everyday life. Everyone, including students, participates by suggesting words to be put into a giant one-line poem or by writing their own poems on the long piece of paper taped around the block.

This was the most enjoyable of all the poetry activities I've participated in. It took place as part of a sculpture festival in Iowa City, and included many "sidewalk sideshows"—that is, street musicians, dancers, theater troupes, and other entertainers. People flocked around all day. Groups of students from several schools and a troop of Girl Scouts came by to ask questions and add their own words.

The day was not without its tense moments. At one point, an older man came out of a tavern and ripped through the paper taped to its façade. He didn't appreciate the esthetics of the situation, so he marched down the street tearing the paper off the walls. "This is a bunch of B.S.," the elderly critic shouted alphabetically as thirty feet of paper rustled on the sidewalk behind him. A friend of mine calmed him down, and he left. The poem continued without any other disruptions.

To make this a really wide-ranging poem, invite all the schools in the area to participate. A multi-school poem can unite students and townspeople in a single creative adventure whose memory will last a long time.

Description

The students and the teacher work together writing a long poem in big letters (up to two feet high) on a sheet of paper taped around a city block. Anyone who passes by can suggest words and ideas for this giant collaboration, and they can write or draw on the paper, too. Plan on a five- or six-hour adventure.

Materials

rolls of white paper (36" wide x perimeter of the block)
felt-tip pens
drawing paper
photocopy machine
posterboard
masking tape
wide, colored felt-tip pens

Preparation

Five or six students tape the paper around the block, cutting it at doorways, alleys, and other areas requiring access. (See "Poem Wrapping the School" for suggestions on acquiring the paper.)

Other things to consider are: picking a good site; obtaining permission from the city and from the businesses whose buildings would be involved; informing the media; making posters; and contacting the state arts council for suggestions and assistance.

Example

This poem wound around the Iowa City block bounded by Dubuque, Washington, and Clinton Streets, and Iowa Avenue. It began:

Poetry City, U.S.A.

Today is all days in the city of words, where the people talk in all the voices under the sun. The sidewalk's crowded with sunny syllables. The sky—so blue it is sad—fills the airplanes with mood music. The lyrics appear in the jet streams. The pilot smiles, flicks on the intercom, says, "Next stop, Poetry City!"

—*Dave Morice and others*

53. POEM COVERING THE GYM FLOOR

This activity makes everyone feel like Gulliver writing an epic in Brobdingnag. When the gym floor is covered with paper, it looks like a giant page. Painting huge words on it is easier than reading them. If the gym has bleachers, the students can go up to the top for a bird's-eye view.

When I used this activity in Trenton, New Jersey, we started writing at one corner of the gym, went all around the outer edge, and continued in a spiral until reaching the center. At the end of the activity, the students had a great time re-rolling the long strips of paper that covered the floor. They were very careful not to tear or crumple any of it. They wanted to save the manuscript for posterity.

Description
The students take turns painting a collaborative poem on paper covering the gym floor. The large letters (two to five feet tall) begin at the outer edge and spiral inward to the center, or vice versa. Every student can suggest words and ideas, but the one who holds the paintbrush has the last word. During this activity, they can make smaller poems and drawings around and within the lines of the big poem.

Materials
rolls of white paper (36" wide), enough to cover the length of the floor in parallel strips
scissors
masking tape
4 quart-bottles of tempera paint (different colors)
2 tempera brushes (1" bristle width)
colored felt-tip pens

Eight to twelve students unroll the paper and tape it over the gym floor. It's a bigger job than wrapping the school. The edges of the paper should overlap by an inch or two.

Alternative

For a one-class activity, unroll a single sheet of paper in the gym from basket to basket. The students write poems anywhere on the paper with the lines trailing in any direction.

Example

In the Gym

[written as a single spiraling line]

In the gym we walk on words to get to the other side. Our footprints will always be here to show where our feet have been wet. We splash the puddles of paint to the end of the poem!

—*Dave Morice and middle school students*

54. HALFTIME POEM ACROSS A FOOTBALL FIELD

Writing a poem across a football field requires teamwork, especially when it's the halftime show at a high school game. The person doing the actual writing has to move fast, and the students have to come up with words and ideas at a rapid rate. A few cheerleaders and an announcer involve the spectators in the writing.

Description

For the halftime show at a football game, the class creates a poem on a piece of paper unrolled from goalpost to goalpost across a football field. The teacher paints the letters on the paper as the students call out words and ideas.

Materials

roll(s) of white paper (36" x 100 yards)
4 cans of spray paint (team colors)

Preparation

Five or six students unroll the paper across the field. If it's windy, other students stand on the edges of the paper to hold it in place.

1) "How are football and poetry alike? How do we score a goal in poetry? Do we need team spirit to write on the field? What is a pass, a field goal, a penalty or personal foul in poetry? Who is the referee?"
2) "What can we write about our team? Do you think we're going to win? What is our biggest strength? And the other team, what is their biggest strength? Can we beat 'em?"

Suggestion

If the halftime is only fifteen minutes or so, the teacher should pace the poem to make sure it's completed. One way to speed up the poem is to paint wider letters.

Alternative

The students take turns writing the poem.

Example

The Rhyming Halftime

[written as a single line]

The game is going like poetry here on the field of Lone Tree. There are many players around these words. They kick the football high as the birds. The goal post tells the team to win. And now it's time to take this page in!

—*Dave Morice and junior high school students*

•

Poetry as a Spectator Sport

A few years ago, Lynn Grulke, the music director at the Lone Tree Community School, asked me if I'd like to teach poetry during the day and write a 100-yard poem during halftime that night at the football game between the Lone Tree Lions and the Morning Sun Tigers. I thought it would be nothing more than that, a poem going across the field. But he had other ideas. To prepare for the event, the band rehearsed a jazzy version of "The Alphabet Song." The cheerleaders practiced some poetry cheers. A team of students volunteered to unroll the paper and hold it in place so the wind wouldn't blow it out of bounds.

That night, at halftime . . . "Metaphor! Metaphor! Tell 'em what we're yelling for!" the cheerleaders shouted at the beginning of the poem. A moment later, I heard: "Hold that line! Make it rhyme!"

Students crowded around and called out words. I spraypainted them in big letters on the long sheet of paper that stretched from one goal line to the other.

It was windier than expected, and volunteers had to come down from the stands to stand on the paper. "Hey! Hey! Dr. A.! How many poems did you write today?" the cheerleaders screamed. "Is that a simile? Yes, it is!" the announcer blared over the microphone to the fans in the stands. "Folks, Dr. Alphabet has just written a simile on the forty-yard line!"

The crowd of 300 or more parents and children watched the action. Everything went smoothly until an unexpected twist almost derailed the poem at the sixty-yard line.

"You're going to have to end it here," a referee said behind me. "There's a league rule that the teams have to be back on the field in fifteen minutes or the game is forfeited. I'm sorry."

"I'll hurry!" I said.

"You've only got two minutes, and then I have to send the teams out onto the field."

The students shouted words for the poem, and I sprayed the letters as fast as I could. We still hadn't finished. Another eighteen yards of paper left. Out of the corner of my eye, I saw both teams rushing onto the field toward the poem—as if they were going to grab it and carry it off the field. Instead, they leaped gracefully over it, stood in formation, and started doing calisthenics.

Relieved, the students and I completed the poem. The wind blew fiercely. A student ran over to the football players and asked if they'd hold up the paper so the fans could see the entire poem. They took positions every six or seven yards and held it up. At the music director's cue, I went over to the microphone in front of the stands and read it aloud. The cheerleaders cheered one last time, and the game resumed moments later.

Lone Tree won. And, thanks to the efforts of many people, poetry crossed the gridiron and scored a touchdown, too. Acting as a team, we wrote one for the Gipper!

55. SPIDERWEB OF WORDS

A ball of twine can change a schoolroom into a completely different place. At Urbandale Junior High, two teachers and I wove twine around a room to make a gigantic spiderweb. When the students came in, they gaped in surprise at the "new look." They had to duck down to walk, and sit on the floor to write. Some chuckled, others gasped. And then they wrote.

This is the first of two activities that alter the writing environment by disrupting part of the room. This disruption creates a "happening" atmosphere, and it makes everyone aware that writing involves a person's entire body and not just the hand, the pencil, and the paper.

Description
The students write poems on irregularly shaped pieces of colored construction paper in a room entwined with twine. As they finish, they tape their poems to the twine. When they're all done, they read them aloud.

Materials
2 balls of twine
Scotch tape (magic transparent type)
colored construction paper
felt-tip pens

Preparation
Three or four students and the teacher move the desks to the side of the room. Then they tie twine to the desks and zigzag it through space—by wrapping it around doorknobs, lacing it through cabinet handles, weaving it among other stable objects, and, if possible, connecting it to the ceiling. The other students wait outside until the room is ready.

Suggested Topic
"Write a poem for a monster movie called, 'The Giant Spider That Devoured (Your School's Name).' Why is it so big? Where did it come from? Who stopped it? How?"

Alternative
While the students write their poems, you write one on a strip of adding machine tape attached to the twine. Your poem is a response from the giant spider's point of view.

Example
There was a spider on the wall. It tried to eat my town.
I studied it very carefully and then I had to frown.
For it was gulping bricks and munching metal, chewing with precision.
After watching for a minute or two, I made my decision.
Splat!

—*Dean Jones, junior high school student*

56. PAPER SKY WRITING

At Southdale School in Cedar Falls, Iowa, we teepeed a room with blue and white crêpe paper. The more we put up, the more it bulged downward like low-hanging clouds. It looked like the sky was falling in thin slices. We had a stack of paper stars, moons, and planets ready for a universe of poems.

A few years ago, contemporary writer David Antin created a work called "Skypoem," skywritten over Santa Monica and La Jolla, California.

Description
The students write on differently colored construction paper cut in the shapes of stars, moons, or planets. They tape the finished poems to a crêpe paper "sky" hanging from the ceiling. Afterwards, they read their poems aloud.

Materials
crêpe paper (blue and white)
Scotch tape (magic transparent type)
black felt-tip pens
colored construction paper (blue and white)

Suggested Topic
"Write a poem for a science fiction movie called, *The Space Creature That Invaded [your school's name]*. What does it look like? Why did it attack the school? How was it defeated?"

Alternative
While the students are writing, you write a poem on adding machine tape hanging with the crêpe paper. Yours is a reply from the space creature.

57. POEMS ON A PUBLIC SCULPTURE

Writing graffiti on a public sculpture is vandalism, but wrapping twine around it and taping freshly-written poems to the twine is perfectly legal. At the end of a twenty-day residency at two schools in Hartford, Connecticut, I obtained a permit from the city for the students and me to write a poem around "The Stegosaurus," a sculpture (a "stabile") by Alexander Calder. Fifty students in fifth and sixth grade at Burns and Mark Twain elementary schools were bussed downtown to "The Stegosaurus." We spent two hours writing poems and taping them to the twine around the dinosaur-sized work. Calder's special love for children and children's toys made his sculpture a perfect place for student poetry.

This activity was a wonderful way for the two schools to work in creative unity. One school had mostly African-American students, and the other had mostly students recently immigrated from elsewhere, including Puerto Rico, Vietnam, and France. Writing the poems together, they got to know each other.

Description
The students write poems on construction paper of different shapes and colors, and then they tape the shapes to twine wrapping a large public sculpture. Afterwards, they read their poems.

Materials
ball of twine
scissors
colored construction paper
strapping tape
Scotch tape (magic transparent type)
black felt-tip pens

Preparation
Three or four students wrap twine around a large public sculpture, circling it enough times to make room for hanging all the students' poems.

Suggested Topics
1) "What does the sculpture look like to you?"
2) "If the sculpture could talk, what would it say?"
3) "If you could make a sculpture for this place, what would you make? What would you name it? What materials would you use?"

58. PAPER CAVE

Caves are mysterious and seductive places. Children in their early years often build caves at home out of chairs and blankets. They enjoy writing on walls, too. This activity gives them a chance to combine these interests by building their own cave and writing poetry on it.

I used this activity with a group of gifted and talented students in Des Moines. Since it was Saint Patrick's Day, we taped light green shamrocks and mushrooms cut out of construction paper to the outside of the cave. They wrote poems on dark green shamrocks, and they collaborated with me on a single longer poem.

The teachers had selected these children for their special interest in poetry. I'd never worked with a group who loved writing as much as they did. Words were their toys. When they came into the room, much of their playground energy seemed to rechannel itself into language. They were unstoppable writers, eager to work on the Paper Cave.

The students build a paper cave in the classroom. Then they write poems on flowers, mushrooms, rocks, stalagtites, stalagmites, bats, and other cave things cut out of construction paper, and tape them inside and outside the cave. The teacher writes a poem with words and phrases dictated by the students.

Materials
scissors
tables
chairs
strapping tape
roll of brown paper (24" x 50')
Scotch tape (magic transparent type)
colored construction paper
black felt-tip pens

Preparation
1) Put three chairs on top of a long table. Tape the feet of the chairs to the tabletop so they don't slide off. Cover the whole thing with strips of brown paper. Then tape the edges of the strips of paper together and tape the strips to the table, chairs, and floor.
2) Cut out pieces of differently colored construction paper in the shapes of things associated with caves.

Suggested Topics
1) "Long ago prehistoric people lived in caves, and they told stories by drawing pictures on the walls. If you were a prehistoric person, what would you put on the walls?"
2) "In the days when pirate ships roamed the seven seas, pirates sometimes hid their treasure in caves. Talk about finding a pirate map that leads to the treasure in a cave. If you found the treasure, what would you do with it?"
3) "If you were a bat living in this cave, what would you do all day? Where would you go to eat? When you came back here at night, would you take your wings off and put on pajamas? What would you watch on TV? What kind of dreams would you have sleeping upside down from the ceiling?"

Example

Shamrock Cave

Shamrocks that blossom on this paper cave
Are printed on their leaves with words of elves.
They talk, they babble in green light, they wave

When the room moves. The people like ourselves
Already see the leprechauns inside.
The leaves of the day are very clever:
There isn't anything too big or wide
To keep the leaves out. (The monsters never
Catch leprechauns by trick or traps—no way!)
The magic ring, imagination's gold,
Will shine upon this world of words today.
That dream is real in lines that will unfold.
So let's crawl in the cave for just a minute
And spend a thousand years traveling in it.

—Dave Morice and third and fourth grade students

59. LIGHTER-THAN-AIR VERSE

A dozen helium balloons can raise poetry to lofty heights. A poem floating skyward harks back to the days of "those daring young men in their
flying machines." Children and adults both enjoy watching the poem
rise like a hot air balloon.

At the Celebration of Abilities in Iowa City, the participants came
up with the words and ideas, and I wrote them down. The festival took
place at the University of Iowa's Carver-Hawkeye Arena. The arena is
more than sixty-five feet high, so I decided in advance that the poem
would end when it reached the ceiling. After three hours, it did. I reeled
the poem in and rolled it up.

Description
The students and the teacher take turns writing a collaborative poem on
adding machine tape. As the poem unrolls, a dozen or so helium balloons carry it ever higher.

Materials
strapping tape
adding machine tape (approximately 3 1/2" x 10')
1/2" dowel rod (approximately 5" long)
string
balloons
tank of helium
wide black felt-tip pens

Preparation
Tie a dozen helium balloons to a dowel rod, and tape one end of a roll
of adding machine tape to it. The balloons should lift the dowel rod and

the adding machine tape. If the balloons don't, add more till they do. Now the poem's ready for lift-off.

1) "What would it be like to fly in a hot air balloon? Where would you go? Who would you see? What would it look like drifting through a cloud? Or floating low above buildings?"
2) "This is our flying word machine. What fuel does it use? Where will it take us? What will we see when we get there?"

Alternative
Two classes participate in a "Poetry Air Race" by writing on separate adding machine tapes. The first tape that runs out of paper wins the race. In case of a tie, the tape with the most words wins.

French artist Jacqueline Monnier has designed kites that go aloft bearing poems about the sky.

Example
At the Nonesuch Fair in Iowa City, this poem was written vertically letter by letter:

> Smile at the Nonesuch Fair because we can have fun dancing on the ceiling! Soon these balloons will get high in the lights and pop! The poem will stop!

60. POETRY CROSSFIRE

It's difficult to listen to two people talking at the same time. One person's words will register for a while, then the other person's. Caught in such a crossfire, the brain sometimes makes odd connections between the two. Such connections can become a natural part of the writing process.

Description
Two students (the readers) sit on opposite sides of a third student (the writer). The first two read simultaneously and nonstop in normal voices from an assortment of picture storybooks or novels. The third writes a poem by catching snippets of what they are reading.

Materials
chairs
picture storybooks or novels
pens
writing paper

Arrange the desks for each three-person group: the writer sits in the middle, and the two readers sit on both sides facing the writer.

61. BLINDFOLD POEM

Writing with a blindfold challenges the student to be creative without all the visual input. For sighted people, it's a completely different experience. Will memory or imagination guide the words?

In 1977 I wrote blindfolded for ten hours at an art festival in New Hope, Pennsylvania. I'd thought that most of the poem would consist of fantasy images, but just the opposite turned out to be true. Since I couldn't see, I was more aware of sounds, smells, and conversations.

The poem was about everything going on around me. People of all ages felt obliged to tell me what was happening in the nearby area. No one suggested I write something fanciful. At one point, a bee landed on the paper and immediately became the topic of everyone's conversation—and earned its fifteen minutes of fame in the poem. Later, when I removed the blindfold after wearing it so long, everything seemed brighter, closer, and flatter until my eyes readjusted.

Description
The students put on blindfolds and write poems by hand for five to ten minutes.

Materials
dark-colored cloth or scarves
black felt-tip pens
writing paper

Preparation
Make blindfolds for the students.

Suggested Topics
1) "What do you hear, feel, and smell? See if you notice anything around you that you didn't notice before."
2) "Describe the darkness. What does it remind you of?"

Suggestion
If the students know how to touch-type, arrange for them to do the activity on typewriters or computers.

62. MYSTERIOUS POETRY BOX

Beyond the curtain in the strangely painted box, an object lies in wait. The student reaches in, feels a curved edge, a furry square, a jagged circle. Part of it seems to be plastic, part metal, part something indefinable. What is in the Mysterious Poetry Box? This is a job for the imagination. Of course, it's a—

Tactile poetry experience! The left hand discovers and the right hand writes about it.

Description
Each student reaches into the Mystery Poetry Box with one hand to feel what is there and writes a poem about what it might be with the other hand. After all the students have written, they read their poems. Then the teacher reveals the object.

Materials
wooden box
scissors
cloth
quick-drying glue
tacks
scissors
paintbrushes
black felt-tip pens
writing paper

Preparation

Stand the wooden box on its side with the open end facing you. Cut two pieces of cloth large enough to cover the box opening. Glue and tack the cloth to the top of the box to make curtains. To make sure the object stays inside the box, nail a board across the bottom of the open side to serve as a guardrail. Paint your own mysterious design on the box, and place a mysterious object inside.

An option: Make an object to put inside the box. Tape, glue, tie, wrap, and otherwise connect smaller objects.

Alternatives

1) Each student makes an unknown object out of other objects at home, and brings it to class in a brown bag or box. Now everyone in class can write about a different object.

2) Write in the dark: one hand writes inside the box, while the other hand waits patiently outside.

CHAPTER 4

WORDPLAY POETRY

*The letters of the alphabet are symbols . . . only a
small number, but combined among themselves, they
form words, poems.*

—Maria Montessori, *From Childhood to Adolescence*

WORDPLAY is one of the ways that children learn to use language.
The sounds of puns, the meanings of riddles, the rhythms of jump-rope
songs—these are natural, enjoyable ways of experiencing words. They
can promote a more positive attitude toward language than do "serious"
sentence exercises, grammar drills, and spelling tests.

In this chapter, students play with words and wind up with poems.
However, writing poetry doesn't have to be the necessary outcome.
Some students may want to do the wordplay alone, and that's worth-
while, too.

The activities appear according to the way words are used—as
single words, sets of words, wordplay forms, and nonsense words. The
chapter concludes with the largest collaborative method in the book.
Such poetry involves two related processes—playing with words and
writing with them.

More than in the previous activities, language itself—rather than an
object, topic, or form—guides the poetry.

63. WORLD'S LONGEST WORD

Creating new words has always been a part of literature. Lewis Carroll
coined a few of his own words, the most well known of which appear
in his immortal poem, "Jabberwocky." James Joyce included many in
his two great novels, *Ulysses* and *Finnegans Wake.*

In this activity, the students work together on a word that is also a
one-word poem having more letters than most regular poems. It offers
the class a chance to get into the *Guinness Book of World Records*, too.
By a liberal estimate, the word would span from 150 to 180 feet of paper and take a total of three to five hours of continuous writing. "The
Longest Word in the World" is a record waiting to be set.

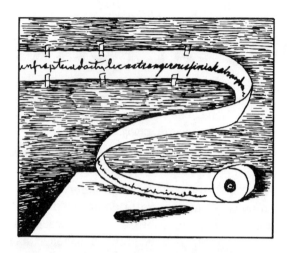

Most importantly, this activity is an enjoyable learning experience for students. They get a sense of team spirit by working together toward a common goal. They enjoy being involved in a project that goes beyond homework and tests and might even make the record book. They feel a sense of achievement as the word grows in length and a sense of anticipation as it reaches completion. They share equally in the success.

Description
The class creates a 10,000-letter word in a single line on adding machine tape taped to the wall of the classroom. This is an ongoing project that lasts throughout the school year. The paper stays up until the word is done. Students add letters whenever they want during their free time.

Materials
Scotch tape (magic transparent type)
roll of adding machine tape
black felt-tip pens
ruler

Preparation
Tape the adding machine tape to a wall. If you can't fit all of it on the wall, tear off segments and use them one at a time. When the word is complete, tape the segments back together.

Suggested Topic
"Our word can have anything in it—stories, names, jumbled-up words and letters. But we do have to follow three rules: first, use letters only—no numbers, commas, dashes, or other things. Second, string the letters together—no spaces. Third, leave mistakes in—no crossing out."

1) When you think the word has passed the 10,000-letter mark, you can count the letters by hand, but it's easy to miscount. Instead, type up the word at fifty letters per line and count the lines instead. At the 200-line mark, the word has 10,000 letters. As a bonus, you have an eight-page transcript. You can photocopy it and give copies to the students. How long does the typing take? At twenty words per minute, one hour and forty minutes.

2) Send a typed version of the word to the *Guinness Book of World Records* along with photos of students working on the handwritten original. Include other documentation, especially any news articles about the word. In the cover letter, signed by you and your students, explain the record, name the participants and location, and request inclusion. But first, contact the editors at least two months before attempting a new Guinness record, to see if they will consider it or not. The address is:

> Guinness Publishing, Ltd.
> 33 London Road
> Enfield, Middlesex
> England.

The 1994 *Guinness Book of World Records* lists the longest words in several languages. For English, it cites a forty-five-letter entry in the *Oxford English Dictionary*, defined as a "lung disease caused by inhalation of very fine silica dust." The word is *pneumonoultramicroscopicsilicovolcanoconiosis*.

•

Words on Making Up Words

What is a word? The preceding question has four strings of letters that everyone would agree are words, but it's not always that clear. Even the dictionaries list things that seem questionable. Is *jack-in-the-pulpit* a word or a group of words? The hyphen makes it a word, but what about the pronoun *no one*? In this case, two words equal one word. Is *TV* a word? *OK*? *BB*? They're all in the dictionary.

The question can't be answered by saying, "These are words; these aren't." As with literature and art, something qualifies as a word if someone says it is. If we tried to define *word*, we would come up with many different definitions. Some would be more inclusive than others, but none would be the ultimate and final one.

A superword of many thousands of letters calls into question the idea of what a word is, especially when the superword's main purpose is to achieve great length. One broad definition that includes such a monster would be "a word is any unbroken string of letters."

Anyone can make up a word of any length—a single letter repeated 10,000 times or a randomly generated string of 10,000 letters. In either case, the result would be boring to most readers. To spice it up, the superword should have more to it. Here are some suggestions to give it flavor and contour:

1) Use a lot of prefixes and suffixes.
PREPOSTNEOANTI- ... ...- INGEDIZATIONISTIC
2) Include the names of everyone who worked on it.
... BILLJACKSONSUSANWHITBYMATTYOSTCAROLYN ...
3) Write poems and stories.
... IWENTTOTHESTORETOBUYFOODBUTITWASCLOSED ...
4) Add a few repeated words.
... TOTOTOTHETHETHETHEMOONMOONMOON ...
5) Add a few random words.
... YELLOWTHISBUGJAMCURTAINASWITHTOOOPAQUE ...
6) Add a few nonsense words.
... SEBBLETONKASPHLEXNOBULAZDAPPAPLATZ ...
7) Put in some repeated letters.
... WWEEFFOOUUNNDDAABBAAGGOOFFMMOONNEEYY ...
8) And some random letters.
... QEROJGERPOKPOJAROWIEJROEGJOREIJGROIEJGREIOJ ...
9) And the alphabet at least once.
... ABCDEFGHIJKLMNOPQRSTUVWXYZ ...
10) And a few sounds to relieve stress.
... EEEEEEEEEEEEYYYYYYYYYAAAAAAAAAHHHHHHHH ...

If you and your students choose to make up a superlong word, good luck! You've got the whole word in your hands.

64. ONE-WORD-A-DAY EPIC

At one word a day, the class has time to really think about what to write. Which word should go in the poem today, *the* or *this*? The tension mounts. The poem becomes a way of marking the calendar. It's a daily reminder of poetry. Students may try guessing tomorrow's word, but no one can be sure until tomorrow.

It's difficult to write at this rate. I tried it on my own, thinking it would be a snap. The poem could go on for years, but I was wrong. For a week, I wrote one word each day, but on the eight day, I forgot. I wrote two on the ninth day to make up for it. As time went on, I forgot to write again and again. It seemed like cheating to write one or two days later, so I gave up after a couple of months.

How long can your class do it without "cheating"?

Description
As a group, the students choose a word a day, and the teacher writes the poem on a piece of posterboard taped to the wall. Only holidays and weekends are exempt.

Materials
white posterboard
Scotch tape (magic transparent type)
black felt-tip pen

Suggestion
Instead of using posterboard, write each word in the appropriate box of a large calendar.

Alternative
A different student gets to pick the word each day.

65. ONE-WORD-PER-STUDENT COLLABORATIONS

This two-day activity is an experiment in individuality. If everyone writes a poem that includes the same set of words, how will the poems differ?

Description
Each student writes one word on a piece of paper, signs it, and passes it in. Next day, you hand out a copy to all the students. They write poems using those words and other words of their own. When everyone's finished, they read the poems out loud to see how differently (or similarly) they handled the list.

Materials
black felt-tip pens
writing paper
typewriter or computer
photocopy machine

Students don't add any words of their own. They assemble the words into a poem as best they can, with standard grammar encouraged but not required.

66. TRICTIONARY

The dictionary lists words in alphabetical order, but concrete poet Ira Steingroot has pointed out that alphabetical order is really random order in disguise. *A* comes first and *Z* comes last for no reason other than that of tradition. Pick out a word at random from the dictionary. Look at the words nearby. Unless they are derived from the same root word, they most likely have no relationship to each other. Trictionary brings them together.

Description
The students each pick a word at random from the dictionary. They copy it, and they also copy the next four main entry words. Then they write a poem using all five words and their own words. They try to follow the definitions even when the words don't seem to go together.

Suggestion
If anyone gets stuck, they can try putting the words in separate sentences.

Examples
The words in these two poems appear in *Webster's Seventh Collegiate Dictionary.*

Nothing

A nothingarian went to sea
Giving orders that were nothingly
They sailed into the nothingness
He was nothing off wearing a dress.

—*Becky Collins, teacher*

Mad

They lost the shipment of mad-
ras on the huge mad-
repores because the crewmen were singing mad-
rigals, sipping mad-
rilenes, and sitting on mad-
ronas.

—*Dave Morice*

67. VOCABULARYCLEPT POEMS

Vocabularyclept? It's a form of anagramming, but whole words are rearranged instead of letters. Wordplay writer Howard Bergerson introduced the idea in 1969. He dissected a poem and published its 478 words in an alphabetical list in *Word Ways* magazine (Word Ways, A. Ross Eckler, Editor, Spring Valley Road, Morristown, New Jersey 07960). Bergerson challenged readers to shuffle the words around to form a new poem. The question was, how much would the two poems be alike?

By using shorter poems of their own, the students can do a similar activity. Even though the same words are used, they usually result in widely different pairs of poems.

This method could fit into either of the next two chapters, but I put it here since it's mostly a development of wordplay. For a similar game poem, see the Poetry Challenge (method 80).

Description

The students write short poems (four to eight lines, twenty to thirty-five words) and the teacher photocopies them onto card stock. Each student cuts out the words from his or her copy and exchanges words with another student. They assemble their new words to make new poems and then copy or glue them on another page. Afterwards, they take turns reading the original poems, followed by the reassembled versions.

Materials

black felt-tip pens
writing paper
white or light-colored card stock
scissors
glue

Suggested Topic

"If you drop a glass, it shatters. What other things shatter? Tell about dropping something or banging into something and making it shatter. Who owned it? Who dropped it? How did it happen?"

Alternatives

1) Each student reconstructs a short poem by a well-known poet and then reads the original and the reconstruction.

2) Same as previous, except all the students have cut-out copies of the same poem. When they're finished, they read their variants.

3) Instead of redoing a whole poem, the students shift all the verbs and nouns to new positions.

4) Instead of words, have them cut out the lines of a poem. Each student then reassembles the lines.

Example

It took me about an hour to transpose the thirty-three words in the first four lines of Shakespeare's eighteenth sonnet to the seven-line stanza below it.

> Shall I compare thee to a summer's day?
> Thou art more lovely and more temperate.
> Rough winds do shake the darling buds of May,
> And summer's lease hath all too short a date. . . .

> Summer's a lovely art.
> May I date thee, darling?
> Thou shall do more
> And compare more, too.
> Shake to the temperate winds,
> And all hath lease of buds.
> Summer's a short, rough day.

68. ANIMAL NAME POEM

Some animal names have other meanings. A bear can't bear to stay awake in winter. Neither a pinto nor a cobra can drive a Pinto or a Cobra. A person can become an Elk, but an elk can't become a person. Puns on animal names abound. Since there is such a large herd of them, they work well stampeding through a student's poem.

The activity is well suited to small groups. The students enjoy coming up with such words. And when they write the poem, they share the merriment of discovering their double meanings.

Description

Each student makes a list of animal names that also mean other things, such as *bear* in "bear market" or "I can't bear it." Then everyone writes a poem with five or more of those words and words of their own to connect them.

Suggestion

As a warm-up, write the double-meaning names of ten animals on the board and ask what they have in common. If no one guesses in a couple of minutes, give them this hint: "Pretend that these aren't the names of animals." If the students still don't know, use a few of the second meanings in sentences.

The students write, using punnable first names of people. For instance, "Pat bills Sue."

Example

Bestiary

The sheepish antelope
horsed around
with a zebra
in his Mustang—
and the bull
couldn't bear it.

The squirrely cat
and his foxy chick
buffaloed a gorilla
who steered his Pinto
into a Cobra—
and the bull
couldn't bear it.

The lion
was pigging out
on a giraffe—

The tiger
wolfed down
an owl—

The elephant
got the moose's
goat—

The turkey
was monkeying around
with a peacock—

The parrot
ratted
on the hens—

and the bull
couldn't bear it
at all!

So he
chickened out
and went ape.

   —*Dave Morice*

69. FOREIGN WORD POEM

Foreign words can be mysterious and exotic. Still, no matter how unfamiliar we are with a foreign word, it always has the power to suggest vague meanings. This activity encourages the search for meaning. In writing Foreign Word Poems, the students make up their own definitions.

To see how it works, try putting these words into sentences: *oni, stijgt, utan, yari*. The translations appear below in A Few Foreign Words to Use.

Teacher Priscilla Alfandre did an interesting project with her third and fourth graders, in which they invented prehistoric languages (see her essay, "Inventing Primitive Languages," in *Educating the Imagination, Vol. 1,* edited by Christopher Edgar and Ron Padgett).

Description
Give each student a different list of four foreign words from four different languages. Everyone discusses the words, makes up pronunciations for them, and comes up with definitions that sound plausible. Then they write poems using the words according to their own definitions. After they're done, reveal the meanings. This activity works well when students divide into small groups to discuss their word lists.

Materials
lists of 4 foreign words
black felt-tip pens
writing paper

A Few Foreign Words to Use

doch = still (German)
oni = they (Czech)
heureux = happy (French)
stijgt = we rise (Flemish)

treni = trains (Italian)
utan = without (Finnish)
verano = summer (Spanish)
yari = his love (Turkish)

aranhuco = huge spider (Portuguese)
blev = was (Swedish)
homme = man (French)
livet = life (Finnish)

mujer = woman (Spanish)
oiseaux = birds (French)
serrare = to clench (Italian)
sogno = dream (Italian)

fiume = river (Italian)
blinkt = shine (Flemish)
mull = earth (Finnish)
grubbel = melancholy (Finnish)

nicht = not (German)
saoul = drunk (French)
som = who (Swedish)
tjockare = thicker (Swedish)

hormiga = ant (Spanish)
ay = moon (Turkish)
ilha = isle (Brazilian)
bocca = mouth (Italian)

occhio = eye (Italian)
glipt = slip (Flemish)
stip = dot (Flemish)
sombre = shadow (Spanish)

Foreign English

Even fairly common words sometimes come from the most exotic places. In *Word Ways* magazine, Maxey Brooke published a list of foreign words that have migrated to English: apartheid (Afrikaans); moose (Algonquin); babble (Akkadian); zebra (Amharic); cumshaw (Amoy); goober (Angolan); henna (Arabic); macaw (Arawak); wombat (Australian); jocko (Bantu); anchovy (Basque); bungalow (Bengali); trek (Boer); hurricane (Carib); mazuma (Chaldean); kaolin (Chinese); pemmican (Cree); labyrinth (Cretan); polka (Czech); skill (Danish); cookie (Dutch); mongoose (East Indian); ankh (Egyptian); kayak (Eskimo); voodoo (Ewe); sauna (Finnish); dock (Flemish); machine (French); slogan (Gaelic); cobalt (German); mercaptan (Greek); pal (Gypsy); canoe (Haitian); ukulele (Hawaiian); cherubim (Hebrew); bandana (Hindu); paprika (Hungarian); whisk (Icelandic); umbrella (Italian); banshee (Irish); kimono (Japanese); frontal (Latin); rattan (Malay); copra (Malayalam); coyote (Nahuatl); shingle (Norwegian); wigwam (Ojibway); bazaar (Persian); alphabet (Phoenician); molasses (Portugese); quinine (Quechua); vodka (Russian); jute (Sanskrit); clan (Scots); cravat (Serbo-Croatian); beriberi (Singhalese); tipee (Sioux);

armada (Spanish); gantlet (Swedish); tattoo (Tahitian); taffy (Tagalog); mango (Tamil); yak (Tibetan); taboo (Tongan); okra (Tshi); tapioca (Tupi); jackal (Turkish); flannel (Welsh); assagi (Zulu).

70. ONE-RHYME POEM

Many students like to rhyme. Although rhyme isn't used often in contemporary poetry, and nowadays children are taught that poetry does not have to rhyme, in some cases the argument for not using rhyme may go too far. In one fifth grade class, I asked the students if they had any general questions about poetry. One girl raised her hand and said in all seriousness, "Can something rhyme and still be a poem?"

I'd never heard that question before. A few times, students have asked, "Do poems have to rhyme?" This activity revels in rhyme carried to an extreme.

Description
Using one of the Lists of Rhyming Words below, the students write poems of eight or more lines, each of which ends with the same rhyming sound.

Materials
photocopy machine
Lists of Rhyming Words (see figure)
black felt-tip pens
writing paper

Preparation
Make photocopies of the Lists of Rhyming Words. Cut out the eight separate lists, and give one to each student.

Alternative
Each student gets two lists and writes a poem dividing the rhymes into alternating lines. In this case, the rhyme scheme is ABABABAB etc.

Examples

Monotony

This lesson is profound.
Sure, someone should be crowned.
Put him in a compound,
To hear his voice resound.
Maybe this will confound
You. Just let me expound.
Each final word must sound

And rhyme, like in a mound
Piled high, above the ground.
It takes more than a pound
Of words to get around
All of those that I found.
My dictionary wound
Them up, to dumbfound
And confuse my hound.
He hunts for a word that's round,
So that it can be bound,
Put into and impound
That will keep and surround
It. Now they all have been downed.
                    "Zounds!"

  —Myldred Strong, PCPO-Sixty

A Tale of Two Trolls

The first troll said, "I'm Rigmarole."
His hand was clenched around a pole.
Behind him stood a female troll.
"I'm Casserole." Her voice was droll.
Her long, thick hair was black as coal.
"Hey, stranger, would you trade your soul,"
Said Rigmarole, "for this rare scroll?"
He pulled it from a pigeonhole
Behind him in a cubbyhole.
My eyes were on the golden bowl
The female held. I had a goal:
To take the bowl from Casserole.
I said, "I'd really rather stroll
Away alone across the knoll."
Just then I saw an armed patrol
Of angry trolls upon the shoal
I heard a bell begin to toll
For me. I felt my nerves unroll
Like coiled snakes, and on the whole
I felt like crawling in a hole.
Instead, I spurred my trusty foal
And, quickly lifting Casserole,
Away, away, away we stole!

  —Dave Morice

•

Lists of Rhyming Words

-ATE	-EEL	-IND	-OZE
ate	deal	bind	bows
bait	eel	dined	clothes
date	feel	find	doze
fate	heel	kind	foes
gate	kneel	lined	froze
hate	meal	mind	goes
late	peel	grind	glows
mate	seal	signed	hose
plate	squeal	whined	nose
rate	steel	behind	owes
slate	wheel	combined	prose
skate	zeal	declined	rose
state	appeal	defined	sews
wait	conceal	maligned	snows
create	ideal	remind	those
debate	reveal	resigned	toes

-AND	-EST	-IP	-OCK
and	best	chip	box
band	chest	clip	blocks
brand	dressed	dip	clocks
canned	guessed	drip	crocks
fanned	jest	flip	docks
grand	messed	grip	flocks
hand	nest	gyp	fox
land	pest	hip	hocks
planned	quest	lip	jocks
sand	stressed	quip	knocks
spanned	test	rip	locks
stand	west	ship	ox
tanned	zest	slip	rocks
demand	confessed	tip	shocks
expand	impressed	trip	socks
withstand	suggest	zip	stocks

71. NUMBER POEM

The students substitute numbers for words. When the writing is nined, each student forty-twos his or her poem aloud, and everyone else twenties to figure out the original eleven (or the new one). If these numbers threw you, read the next section.

Description
The students write poems by replacing words with numbers whenever they want. The numbers should be made plural or put in the past tense, just like the original words. When everyone is finished, each student reads his or her poem aloud, and everyone tries to figure out the original meaning (or the new one).

Suggested Topics
1) You're on a space shuttle. A voice comes over the loudspeaker: "Ten, nine, eight . . . ." Write about the flight, using words and numbers in your poem.
2) You've just had a math class, and your head is full of numbers. You want to tell someone about a movie or TV show you like, but the numbers keep coming up in your speech.

72. PUN NAMES

To pun is to have fun. Children, in their linguistic innocence, laugh at puns with reckless abandon. Adults enjoy puns, too, but often wince, act disgusted, or feign throwing up in response. The pun, in spite of its bad reputation, is the most widely used and widely abused form of wordplay in English.

In this activity, names are punned into phrases that become lines of poems. There is one guiding principle behind the list: any name can be made into a punning word, phrase, or sentence. When students realize this, they learn one of the secrets of language.

Description
The students read untitled copies of the List of Presidential Pun Names and try to figure out whose names are being punned upon. If they can't find the answer, start reading the phrases aloud.

After that introduction, the class writes poems using five or more pun names. They can pick them from the list or they can make up some new ones from other famous people. The pun names function as individual lines that need more lines to tie them together.

photocopy machine
List of Presidential Pun Names (below)
black felt-tip pens
writing paper

Preparation
Make photocopies of the List of Presidential Pun Names (below) and hand them out.

Alternative
Each student writes three or more four-line poems using different pun names for titles.

List of Presidential Pun Names
(Photocopy this list without its title.)

George watching dawn	Grow fair, cleave land
John had hams	Been jammin', hairy son?
Tom has chef for son	Grow fair, cleave land
Shame's maddest son	Will ya, Mick? Can Lee?
Chains, men. Row!	The odor Rosy felt
John, quints see autumns	Wool yam? How, er, daft
Ann drew Jack's son	Wood! Row well, son
Marred in ban, viewer ran	Warn hard. Ding!
Will ya, men, rehearse son?	Calf in cool itch
John, dial her	Her bird? Who? Fur
Gem's cape oak	Frank? Lynn? Della? No, Rosa felt
Sack hairy tailor	Hairy? Yes! True, man
Milord, fill more	To wide day, fit eyes in hour
Frank, lean peers	John fits chair, old kin, Eddie
Dames view cannon	Land on bee. John's on
A bra hem—link on	Rich yard nicks sun
Ann drew John's son	Cherry Ford
You lease ease. Yes, grand	Shimmy garter
Rudder for bee haze	Run, old Dragon!
James, a car field!	Charge! Push!
Jester, eh, author?	Bilk lint on

73. PERSONAL ANAGRAM POEMS

Ocean and *canoe* are anagrams. If you switch all the letters of one around, you can spell the other. Anagrams go back thousands of years, and they appear in most languages. Satires, religious texts, and even magical writings have used anagrams. The appeal of the form lies in its clever simplicity.

Description

The students print their first and last names on a sheet of paper. For about five minutes, they make complete or partial anagrams by spelling words with the letters in their names. Then they write poems that include ten or more of those words.

Suggestion

Some students may have names that are especially difficult to anagram. If they can't make ten, they should use the words they find. Or they can try anagramming the name of a parent, a relative, or a friend.

Alternative

Anagram the name of a famous person you admire, and write a poem about him or her.

Examples

The first two poems mix partial anagrams with other words.

> She was born one fall day
> On the brink of a rill
> Nature became her closest of kin.
> When danger would fill the air
> She ran to a barn nearby.
> There she might roll in the hay.
> Time passed quickly—she became frail.
> She would blink her eyes;
> Soon sleep would come forever.
>
> *(Fan, fill, lair, nab, knob, flair, rib, ink, link, brink, rail, fin, nor, rink, an, nail, rill, lay, frill, in, fall, bin, air, blink, roll, ran, ray, ban, boil, of, frail, barn.)*
>   —Fanny Ilonka Blair, PCPO-Sixty

> Yes My Darling
> I'll always see a
> way and meaning
> in all my dreams
> I saw you in a
> Middy Dress and
> as a Lad I sang
> daily and ran
> as I went waring
> Ye added Gild and

Jade in my ward
Smiling at me
Darling all I want
is, Let me hear
ye say, I'll always
miss hearing ye
dear Laddie.
War ended and
Laddie was already
sailing at Sea
Ned & Dean saw
Laddie sailing in Lady's
Den smiling as always
& Jennie Wren singing
Yes My Darling Gladie Jane

—Gladys Edwards, PCPO-Sixty

The last poem uses partial anagrams all the way. The student added no other words.

A Cool Brook Lea

O! Look! roe leap' a cool lea,
A lark call o' brook ba' -bl, lap, race.
Lo, Bo Peep! lace cloak, cape - all.
A creap rob' Bo Peep' Crook.
People care - peal a bell.
Creap leap' the creek.
Cop rap' creap - clap back o' bar'
Bo Peep bake' cake - rope' ace cop.
People lap coke, cool.

(Author's note:The next time I do this I will add Miss next to my name to provide some s's.)

—Cora Belle Pollock, PCPO-Sixty

•

Anagrams and Antigrams

Good anagrams relate in meaning to each other: *canoe* relates to *ocean*. But when they have opposite meanings, they are called "antigrams." Some of the best anagrams and antigrams ever written in English appear below. There are twenty-six examples of each.

Most of them first appeared in *The Enigma* or *The Eastern Enigma*, two publications of the National Puzzlers' League (NPL). If you want to see a few more, see *The New Anagrammasia*, edited by Ross Eckler (Spring Valley Road, Morristown, NJ 07960, $15). Containing 8,876 anagrams and antigrams published between 1797 and 1991, it's the largest collection in any language.

Anagrams

the active volcanos—cones evict hot lava
anagrams—ars magna
a bartender—beer and art
a decimal point—I'm a dot in place
desperation—a rope ends it
a divorce suit—I advise court
dormitory—dirty room
driveway—yard view
edge tools—good steel
execution—exit on cue
Galahad—had a gal
gold and silver—grand old evils
greyhound—hey, dog, run
HMS Pinafore—name for a ship
limericks—slick rime
moonlight—thin gloom
the nudist colony—no untidy clothes
old masters—art's models
pittance—a cent tip
prosperity—is property
schoolmaster—the classroom
television news—it's now seen live
unadorned—and/or nude
woman scorned—now man scored
X-rated movies—video sex mart
yodelling—dog yellin'

Antigrams

Anheuser Busch—shun such a beer!
antagonist—not against
customers—store scum
a diet—I'd eat

deanship—pinheads
diplomacy—mad policy
dormitories—tidier rooms
earliest—rise late
epitaphs—happiest
filled—ill-fed
forty-five—over fifty
funeral—real fun
giant—gnat, I
honestly—on the sly
inferno—non-fire
lemonade—demon ale
maidenly—men? daily
medicate—decimate
militarism—I limit arms
nominated—not named
persecuted—due respect
roast turkey—try our steak
Roosevelt—vote loser
the ship Titanic—hasn't hit ice tip
the winter gales—sweltering heat
within earshot—I won't hear this

74. ANAGRAMARAMA

Suppose a student wants to do more anagram poems? Here's an activity you can give as take-home writing. The student can read the finished work to the class.

Description
The student makes up a phrase or line to begin the poem. All the remaining lines are complete anagrams of the first line (and of each other). The easiest way to do this is to slide letter tiles (Scrabble or homemade) to create new lines. The poem doesn't have to rhyme, but the anagram form makes rhyming easy to do. Phrases of twelve to twenty-five letters work best.

Suggestions
1) Longer sentences (thirty letters and up) have more possible anagrams, but working with lots of letters takes more time. A good short phrase can be just as effective and less confusing.
2) Sentences with the letters *j, q, x,* and *z* will be the most difficult to anagram.

3) Sentences with a lot more vowels or a lot more consonants are usually more difficult than sentences with a fifty-fifty split.
4) Sentences with few *e*'s can be tricky.
5) Avoid using made-up spellings of words (like *u* for YOU) or abbreviations. Anagrammatists consider this a cop-out. Oh well, go ahead.

Example
The phrase, "the missing link," is surprisingly easy to anagram. To make this poem, I first assembled a few anagrammed lines and tried them out in different arrangements in order to give the poem as much meaning and coherence as possible.

Song of the Missing Link

Think! Sing, Slime!
Slime's thinking.

Sink, Slime Thing,
Set him slinking.

Night's ink! Slime
Lets him, sinking

Slime Thing's kin:
Helm is stinking.

Sing! Think slime!
Slime's thinking.

In writing the poem below, I "loaded" the starting sentence with specific letters in order to spell *Tinman, Witch, Lion, Wizard,* and *Toto.* Because of line length, meaning, and rhyme, the poem took several hours to write. Students may wish to take such an approach, but it's not necessary.

Dorothy Was Once in the Emerald City of Oz

Dorothy was once in the Emerald City of Oz:
She tried the way to Oz, forced in many cool
Woods nicely on the road for the city maze.
The icy dew froze Tinman. "Choose a dry tool,"

He said more wretchedly. "Oof! Tin not a cozy
Coat now. My foot dozes there, Child, in year."
"Try oilcan of Oz," Dorothy said. "Hence we met."
The Witch: "No freedom do I slay, no cozy tear."

"Come on, stay! For they lionized the coward."
Yonder the crazy Witch made Lion's foe, too,

Doom his tail. Toy, chore, or zany new defect?
A mean old Witch cried to Oz, "Try on fey shoe."

Wizard said to her, "Come! Only fetch yon toe!
If Lion cared, who do they center at my zoos?"
Then hot, moody Scarecrow failed yet in Oz.
They fed Scarecrow hay. "No, don't limit ooze."

Scarecrow moaned, "They fly into Oz to hide.
Raze homey castle door." Din of witchy tone!
O, Holy Tinman recorded size of way to etch
Secret of Wizard: "Hi-ho! Today note my clone."

Dorothy wanted more in life: "O, yes, Oz. Catch
My Toto!" She realized why no force can do it.
"O, Em is not here!" Dazed with act of loony cry,
Dorothy had zest. "Crone! Felon! Me? I, a coy wit."

O, Scarecrow! O, Tinman! O, Oz! They hid, yet fled.
O, Moon! Fate! Cry only zero. The Witch is dead!

75. SOUND POEM

Sound poets often take language to an extreme. They have composed long, elaborate poems without any "meaning" other than the sound of the words. In this respect, sound poems resemble music. Notable sound poets include Kurt Schwitters, Hugo Ball, Velimir Khlebnikov, and Henri Chopin. American poet Michael McClure used a lot of sound words in his book *Ghost Tantras*.

Description
Each student writes a poem using sound words. They can be dictionary words such as *bang* and *crash*, or they can be brand new sounds such as *oooo-agghhhhh*. They can represent a specific scene or situation, such as a car crash, or they can just sound good together. After the writing, the students read their poems, and the other students interpret the sounds.

Suggestion
Before the activity, discuss sound words like those in comic books (*wham, bop, crash, zoom*) with students. They can use them in the poem along with their own sound words.

Example
The author of this poem is a sound poet, not a student.

GRRR!

Wham! Pow! Zinnnnnnnnng!
Oof! Boing boing boing
Boing—click!

Shhhhh!

Mmm! Ugh! Wheeeeeeeee—bonk!
Whoosh zip whoosh zoom
Hisssssssssss! Arfarfarf!

Shhhhh!

Arf!

—Joyce Holland

76. GIBBERISH

To write gibberish poems, you have to think in a parallel linguistic dimension. It's not too difficult. You pretend that you're saying something, but the words are not English. Where do they come from? Only the subconscious knows. Gibberish is the ultimate form of speakable nonsense.

Lewis Carroll's "Jabberwocky" is nonsense that almost makes sense. He invented many of the words in it: "'Twas brillig, and the slithy toves / Did gyre and gimble in the wabe. / All mimsy were the borogroves, / And the mome raths outgrabe." The poem succeeds partly because of its nonsense words.

Description
Everyone writes a poem entirely of invented words about any topic or no topic at all. When the students read their poems, they put as much feeling into them as they would if they were in plain English. After the reading, the class discusses possible meanings.

Suggestions
1) Students may alter the rules; for example, a few may simply write real words backwards.
2) Students may want to write translations next to the poems.

Alternative
Two students alternate in writing a gibberish telephone conversation. After the writing, both students read their parts, and the other students try to guess what they are talking about.

The Cat

Eht yzarc tac
Llef ni eht revir
Eh dluoc ton miws
Os eh deklaw tuo

—*Myldred Strong, PCPO-Sixty*

tishie dishie	Little dish
rea gea	Are green peas
hepper shakie	Be a pepper shaker
rable tound	Are you on a round table

—*Nellie Voelckers, PCPO-Sixty*

Arok Truden

Quiddily que Dee Dee
Hodily fee bee we
Rodily ja do goo
Madjo po tally foo.
Pake toesy tral tee
Whan poesh whampee
Arok truden Ulob Ulob
Geg mit se me fash chob
Whank Twigit Tom som
Quee Hoko Pa thom.

—*Cora Pollock, PCPO-Sixty*

No Meaning

nutsboye oggloy utsna oybry
irlg riendf oyb otherm aids
rassg si reeng ni prints
teh irdsb ings ni prints
teh kys si lueb ni het prings

—*Clarice Stenby, PCPO-Sixty*

77. RUBBER STAMP POEMS

In recent years, rubber stamp art has become a popular genre. It's an amusing and inexpensive kind of art that anyone can do. Similarly, poetry can be created using rubber stamps, and in an endless variety of ways. In this activity, students make concrete poetry pictures with alphabet stamps.

Each student makes pictures by stamping letters of the alphabet on a sheet of paper. Then he or she stamps the first line of a poem about the picture on the same page and writes the entire poem on a separate page.

Materials
rubber stamp alphabets
stamp pads
drawing paper
pens
writing paper

Suggestions
1) For best results, always use high quality stamps and indelible ink pads. Cheap stamps with colorful sponge pads and washable ink give washed-out results and fall apart quickly.
2) For further ideas on the use of rubber stamps in making art, look into *The Rubber Stamp Album* by Joni K. Miller and Lowry Thompson.

Alternatives
1) The students each pick a word, such as *cat*, and use only those letters in making the picture.
2) They use a single letter only, or many random letters.
3) They use other rubber stamps—personal stamps, mass-market stamps, and business stamps—to make the picture.

78. ALL-SCHOOL COLLABORATION

Everyone—students, teachers, principal, librarian, janitor, bus drivers—who works at school can work on this poem. The trick is to get the whole school to participate. The resulting collaboration is a patchwork quilt of handwriting and poetry.

Description
To start the poem, you write a line and sign your name after it. Then each of your students writes a line and signs it. After that, the poem, along with an explanatory letter, goes around the school. Everyone from principal to custodian can participate. Non-writers can dictate their lines. When the poem is finished, display a copy in the media center or print up copies for everyone.

Materials
spiral notebook
black felt-tip pens
letter of explanation (see sample below)

School Collaboration Poem
(Sample letter of explanation)

Your name
Grade
Homeroom number

Dear Participant:

The School Collaboration Poem is a writing project in which everyone in the school can participate. It takes very little time. Here is all I would like you to do:

1) Read the last three or four lines of the poem.

2) Write one line of your own after the last line. The line should be made up on the spot.

3) Sign your name in the left-hand margin.

4) Pass this letter on, or return it to me.

You may write whatever you want—serious, humorous, sensical or nonsensical. Your line can be as long or as short as you want.

When everyone, including students, faculty, and staff, has put a line in, I will make copies of the complete poem for all the people who took part. [Or: I will display the complete poem in the media center.]

Thank you.

Sincerely,

_____

CHAPTER 5

GAME POETRY

Every poem should be like
A game of pinball.

—Allan Kornblum, "The Pinball Manifesto"

LIKE WORDPLAY, gameplay can be an effective learning tool. Games teach many things, such as cooperation, competition, negotiation, strategy, prediction, logic, and of course game-playing. Most students are familiar with game boards, cards, and dice. The familiar pleasure of games can be transferred to poetry.

In some ways, poetry is a game. The words are pieces, and the object is to write a poem. The poet makes up the rules, which are founded on language, and the poet plays the game. One general rule applies to these poetry games: The words should form grammatically correct sentences. This is not meant to test a student's knowledge of English, but to ensure that the resulting lines of poetry cohere at a basic level. The structure of a sentence transmits meaning even when the words are the result of random selection.

There are two kinds of game poetry. In solitaire games, the students use game pieces to write poetry, but no competition is involved. Everyone who plays wins. Poetry Poker (below) is a good example of a solitaire game. In competitive games, two or more students play by rules to win the game and make a poem at the same time. In this case, the poem acts as a means of keeping score. Poetry Challenge and Poetry Scrabble fit into this category. Alphabet Dice and Poetry Checkers have variations that fall into both categories.

In this chapter, each listing starts with a Rules section that specifies the number of players. The entire class writes with the solitaire games, but only a few students at a time can play the competitive games. I suggest making the latter available on request.

79. POETRY POKER

Poetry cards in the classroom? Poker with poetry? The very thought of it catches the students' attention. It's easy to do, it's quick, and it's fun. For those (and other) reasons, I've used this activity in almost every class I've taught. More than 5,000 students from nine to ninety-six have played the game and won—a poem.

This activity helps break the ice to get to the flowing waters of the imagination. It melts away any preconceived notions the students might have about poetry. When they see the cards, they don't know what to say. So they write instead.

They write amazing poems with funny metaphors, haunting images, long rhyming narratives, short free-verse quips, and surprise endings. They play the game with gusto. After all, no one really knows what a good Poetry Poker hand is.

Rules (1 player)
Object: To write a poem that includes the phrases typed on five Poetry Poker cards. The teacher deals five cards to each student. The students read the phrases on the cards and arrange them in any order they like. Then they write individual poems using all five phrases and many of their own words to connect them. They can alter the phrases grammatically to fit their poems.

Optional Rules: 1) Discard—If the student doesn't like a card, he or she can exchange it for another. 2) Trade—Students sitting next to each other can trade cards to improve their hands.

Note: Make sure that the students know they should use lots of their own words. When I use this method, one or two students inevitably try to make poems out of the phrases alone.

Materials
decks of poker cards
typewriter
black felt-tip pens
writing paper

Preparation
Make one or more decks by typing phrases on regular poker cards. Refer to Marking the Cards (below) for a sample list of phrases.

Alternative
The students write very short poems, a dozen words or fewer, directly on the cards.

Examples
In the examples that follow, I've tried to show some of the great variety of poems that students in different classes and ages have written. The writers include upper elementary students, an undergraduate student, teachers, and older people.

Old Train

I saw the old train
go off the track
With an extra truck
stacked on back.

—Lori Henry, upper elementary

I invited my friend over. When she
came she stood at the door and
she looked like she was scared to
knock. So I yelled out the window
it's okay to knock. She knocked
and the roof fell off. My father
yelled "Yeah! the roof is falling."
So we had to move to the forest.
We saw a sign in the forest. It
said "here's how to growl." We
didn't pay attention to it. Then
I saw a neat tree to climb. I
started to climb it and fell. My
dad said "you'll never be able to
climb that tree." I started to
climb the tree. I yelled to my
dad "I'm climbing."

—Shan, upper elementary

The Witch of Time

The witch of time was made of goober and slime.
She was red, white and green and very obscene
and made from the time of a caveman in green.
She said make it a good one for the stove bursts
into or I'll take a piece of your nose
and throw it away with the old rotten hose.
My mouth went dry as the flame grew high,
but the old witch of time who was goobery and slimy
went away with the grimys.

—Irene, upper elementary

Once upon a time I saw it fly loudly the zebras. I love the loudly of the
zebras. One day I heard my mom say make it a good one. I love the way
it flies. It flies loudly like the zebras. I love it when you make a good one.
One day me and my friend went to the loudly zebras. It flies and it makes
me feel like a good one. It makes me feel good.

—Tammy Burr, upper elementary

Behind the comet is
the evil factory looking
at the things everybody
needs.

—Doris Strable, upper elementary

One Halloween we were going to have a party in the old Simpson house.
There was one thing wrong. There was a big piece of cheese on the roof.
It was balancing when we were inside and the roof leaked with acorns.
Then too few plants leaked. Someone threw an apple at the cheese and the
house caved in.

—Scott Schultz, upper elementary

Welcome home mama. Hurry stop the
table. It tripped on your shoes. And it's falling. My
toenails are flashing. I'm climbing on my mother's back.
But my motorcycle is doing the
laundry where the bats fly.

—Phillip Clow, upper elementary

You destroy asking faces
Comfort them with peaches now
Hear keys clicking from the dog's chain
Comfort them with peaches now
Peaches bright and juicy
Questions fade away
Peaches cool and sweet
Fears put in the shade

—Kristine Weidel, undergraduate

Noises

The collie sleeping soundly
Snoring a song with flies buzzing all around
Makes me cry, as I look through the apple
Made of glass at lunch time.

—Jan Blankenburg, teacher

Yes, You

The clever plants knew—yes, you
You were a phony ant
The zebras knew if they chased rabbits

Yes, you were fast rabbits
  Loudly the zebras ran to the clever plants
Yes, you were their choice for lunch.

  —*Sharon Pilling, teacher*

Morning in Wonderland

The long grass softly blows on the
Side of the hill
Creating warm feelings across
My heart's door.
I can see dew on each blade
Though there is no sunlight.
I love the fresh morning air
And the hatfuls of snow that
I picked at dawn.

  —*Elissa Swafford, teacher*

Could a clock make time
In a telephone booth?
Its eyelashes, like so many umbrellas,
Fluttering in joy over its swooning white eyes.
Remember how you ruined it all
by looking at your watch?

  —*Chris Dutson, teacher*

Departure

A sleek silver ship
Sails slowly beneath the bridge.
The top of the water gleams
As the sailors lose sight of home,
And look toward the home of their daydreams.

  —*Judy Slobodnik, teacher*

Magic

Such magic in the house
Such magic in the telephone booth
Don't listen to the glasses & cups
Don't listen in the house
I've found it: such magic!

  —*Pearl Minor, PCPO-Sixty*

Here are some short poems written with the Alternative method:

parrot, who replies I don't want a cracker I want pies
  —*Nellie Voelckers, PCPO-Sixty*

  The
          Leaf
                  Kept
turning the corner
  —*Fanny Blair, PCPO-Sixty*

  Too many moons
In my pantaloons
  —*Myldred Strong, PCPO-Sixty*

Marking the Cards

Each card has a phrase of two to four letters typed across the center (or the top in the case of picture cards). The words could be written with pen and ink, but typewritten words maintain the look of an "official" deck.

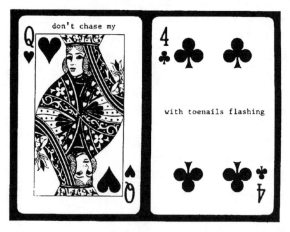

The selection of phrases is important. They determine in part what the students write. This list has fifty-four phrases divided into three categories. The complete phrases have self-contained ideas that sound fairly normal. The incomplete phrases begin or end mid-thought and require completion. The unusual phrases are complete, but they have a surrealistic twist to them.

Most of these words come from four decks that I've used with many different ages and classes.

Complete Phrases	Incomplete Phrases	Unusual Phrases
to the store	without the new	magic hamburgers
eating fish	jumped off the	with toenails flashing
stale piece of pie	gold as the dome of	a dinosaur or two
a pretty face	it was going	1,000 pianos
I promise	smashed between	beautiful blue teeth
all the flags	in this tired	asking faces
red paint	knowing who	mouthful of bees
the spaceships	the house as another	the evil factory
old train	oh, no, I	how to growl
a stereo	don't chase my	apples as gray as
I would like	cheese and	sloppy hippos
the roof leaked	up the puzzle	stop the table
banana split	the flags	to laugh slowly
going crazy	without her nice old	round eggs
the pickle jar	wherever the goat	phony ant
a balloon pops	spins the wheel	zoo monster
my stomach	almost got hit	color of sleep
no sunlight	saw a hotdog	snoring a song

80. POETRY CHALLENGE

Which student can outpoem the other? The pieces are words, the rules are simple, but the game is a challenge.

Rules (2-4 players)
Object: Each player lays down word tiles to form a collaborative poem with the other player or players. The students write poems, and the teacher copies them onto card stock. Students playing against each other should have differently colored copies. They each cut out twenty-five words from their copies to make word tiles for the game.

Example: In a two-player game, Player A lays down a word that begins a sentence, and Player B lays down a word to the right of the first word to continue the sentence. Play continues with each player adding a word to the right of the previous word. When a sentence ends, the next player starts a new line. If a player can't add a word, he or she must pass.

Scoring: The game is over when a player uses all of his or her words or when neither player can continue the poem. To determine who wins, the players count their color tiles. The player who has used the most tiles (and thus words) is the winner.

Materials
colored construction paper
scissors
black felt-tip pens

Suggested Topic
For the written poems: "Compare life to a game you're familiar with, like Monopoly or chess. Who are the players? How do you win? What is one important rule? Why?"

Alternatives
1) Sudden death variation: if a player cannot play a word, he or she loses. The game ends when only one player is left—the winner.
2) A player lays down a new word on top of any word already in the poem. The "rewritten" sentence must still be grammatically correct.

81. ALPHABET DICE

Many board games use dice. In this game, the boards are sheets of paper for writing poetry. The chance roll of Alphabet Dice guides the choice of words.

Rules (2–4 players)
Object: Each player makes a poem by writing one line on each toss of the Alphabet Dice. Two players take turns rolling five alphabet dice. At every roll, all the players write a line of poetry composed of words beginning with the letters on the dice. The players can arrange the letters in any order, and they don't have to use all the letters. However, their lines should be gramatically correct.

Scoring: After both players have rolled the dice eight times and written up to sixteen lines, the game is over. The players count the letters and the syllables in their words and add them up. They subtract five for every line with a grammatical error. High score wins.

Example: In a two-player game, player A throws LPTTO. He changes the order to TOTPL and writes "The old turtle plods lightly." Player B decides on a different order, LOPTT, and she writes "Long orange peach trees touch." Player A's line scores 24 letters + 7 syllables = 31 points; player B's line scores 25 letters + 5 syllables = 30 points.

Three players take five turns each for a fifteen-line poem; four players take four turns for sixteen lines.

Materials
black felt-tip pens
writing paper
alphabet dice (from the game of Boggle or from another source)

Alternative
Random Acrostic Method: Instead of playing a game, the student writes a poem by rolling the dice to determine the first letter of each line. This works well with assigned topics.

82. MENTAL BLOCK

When writers get a mental block, they have to stop writing for a while. Something has blocked the words. In this game, the words form their own mental block, which forces one of the players to stop writing and end the game. However, both players write several lines before reaching a mental block, and those lines make their poems.

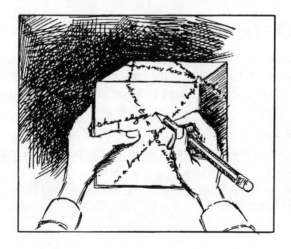

Rules (2-4 players)

Object: To write poetry one line at a time across the sides of a cube. Player A starts by writing a line from one edge to the other on any side. Player B does the same on the opposite side of the cube. Then Player A writes his second line starting at the point on the edge where his first line ended. The new line goes across the new side.

As play continues, the players observe the following rules:

1) Crossings—The player tries to write lines that cross the opponent's lines. Each crossing is worth one point. Players should keep track of crossings on a separate piece of paper.

2) Closed sides—A player cannot write on a side that has two lines of his or her own already on it.

3) If a player winds up on an edge that leads to a closed side, he or she can't move any more. The other player continues writing until he or she winds up at a closed side.

4) At that point (when neither player can move), the game is over.

5) The player who has made the most crossings is the winner.

Preparation

Find or make boxes measuring roughly four to eight inches per side. They should have a clean, light surface.

Suggested Topics

1) "Write about not being able to write. What are some of the things you aren't writing about? Why aren't you writing about them?"

2) "You're walking your pen around the block—the Mental Block, that is. Write about your pen as if it were a pet. What would you feed it? Where would it sleep at night? What tricks can it do? How does it show that it likes you?"

83. POETRY SCRABBLE

Scrabble is one of the most popular board games in the world. It challenges players to form words on the crossword-like board, but the words have no rhyme or reason except to score points. In this variation, the reason is poetry.

Rules (2-4 players)

Object: To use Scrabble tiles to form a collaborative poem with the other player(s).

Poetry Scrabble follows the standard Scrabble rules, with some simple and clear changes:

1) The players divide all the tiles at the beginning of the game and lay them face up in front of them.

2) They may form words up to eight letters in length, but no longer than that.

3) The first player must make a word that normally begins a sentence. Every word after that has to continue the poem by forming grammatically correct sentences. If a player uses a word that doesn't work, he or she must remove it from the board and forfeit the turn.

4) On each turn, the player has to connect his or her word to the previous word added to the poem.

5) If a player plays a word that connects to two or more words on one turn, both count toward the score, even if only one of them continues the poem. If more than one continues the poem, the next player is free to choose which one to use in connecting the next word.

6) Scoring is the same as in regular Scrabble, except there is no fifty-point bonus for playing seven tiles. To keep track of the poem and the score, draw three lines down a sheet of paper. On each player's move, write the word played (and thus added to the poem) in the middle column and the score in the player's column, like this:

PLAYER A	POEM	PLAYER B
34	| THIRSTY |	
	| BEAGLES |	18
16	| FADE |	

Materials
black felt-tip pens
writing paper
Scrabble game set

84. POETRY CHECKERS

Poetry Checkers offers lots of writing possibilities. You can use it to generate a sentence automatically. You can write a poem and play a game of checkers at the same time. Or you can try other ways.

On the Poetry Checkerboard (see figure), the light squares have four words apiece. By moving a checker from square to square, you can form many different sentences. The teachers in my Alternative Poetry Writing Class found the Poetry Checkerboard to be highly versatile. They came up with their own methods, which I've listed in the Alternatives by Teachers section below. Their poems and comments appear in the Examples section.

Object: Each player writes a poem based on the moves he or she makes on the Poetry Checkerbord. During the game, the players "capture" words as described below and use each word in a line. At the end of the game, the player with the most lines wins. (Note that a player may win the regular checkers game but lose at Poetry Checkers by writing a shorter poem.)

Players capture words by moving, jumping, and kinging:

Moving—On completing a move, the player chooses one of the four words in the square that his or her checker now occupies.

Jumping—On jumping an opponent's checker, the player chooses a word from the square occupied by the jumped checker.

Kinging—On reaching the king's row, the player chooses two words from the square with his or her checker on it—one for moving to that square and one for kinging.

Materials
photocopy machine
red card stock
The Poetry Checkerboard (see figure)
scissors
black felt-tip pens
writing paper

Preparation
Photocopy (and enlarge) the Poetry Checkerboard onto red card stock.

Alternative
Zigzag method: Form sentences automatically with the Checkerboard by picking a side and turning the board so that side becomes the top row. Pick a square in that row, zigzag down in regular checker moves, and read the top word in each square. All eight words make a sentence. The lines range from the perfectly normal ("We read books but watch movies at night") to the bizarre ("We plant cats that grow leaves in barns")—both of which begin with the "We" square.

Alternatives by Teachers
In my Alternative Poetry Writing Class, a graduate course for teachers, I handed out copies of the Poetry Checkerboard and described the zigzag method for making sentences on it. The students (teachers) commented that the Checkerboard could probably be used in a lot of other ways. I asked them to use it however they wanted. To my surprise, all of them came up with different ways. Here are the methods they came up with, followed by some of their poems and comments.

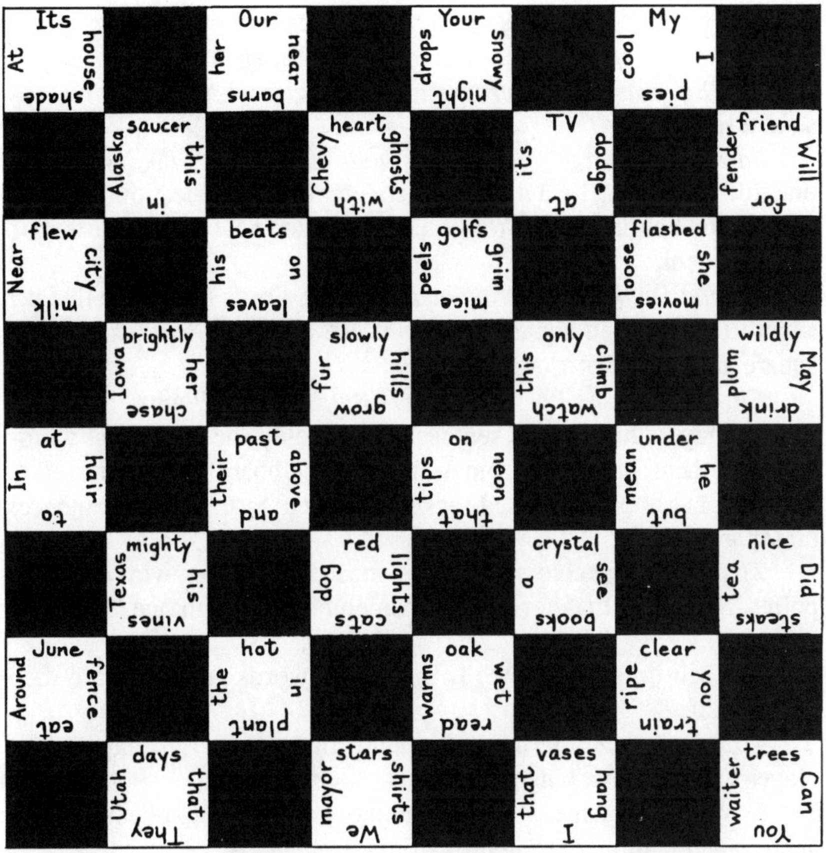

Grid (each cell shows its four words: top / left / right / bottom):

Its / At / house / shade	Our / her / near / barns	Your / drops / snowy / night	My / cool / I / said
saucer / Alaska / this / in	heart / Chevy / ghosts / with	TV / its / dodge / at	friend / fender / Will / for
flew / Near / city / milk	beats / his / on / leaves	golfs / peels / grim / mice	flashed / loose / she / knows
brightly / Iowa / her / chase	slowly / fur / hills / grow	only / this / climb / watch	wildly / plum / May / drink
at / In / hair / to	past / their / above / and	on / tips / neon / that	under / mean / he / but
mighty / Texas / his / vines	red / dog / lights / cats	crystal / a / see / books	nice / tea / Did / steaks
June / Around / fence / eat	hot / the / in / plant	oak / warms / wet / read	clear / ripe / you / train
days / Utah / that / They	stars / mayor / shirts / We	vases / that / hang / I	trees / waiter / Can / you

Charlene Engstrom's alternating lines method: Make the first line by row selection. Write the second line using your own words. Continue by repeating those two steps, alternating the checkerboard word lines and your own lines. Use a different row each time.

Judy Slobodnik's alternating lines method: Pick a row. Make the first line by square selection using words in the first square in the row. Write your own second line. Continue those steps, but go to the next square each time.

Becky Collins's first-and-last-line method: Make two lines by square selection. Use them as the first and last lines of the poem. Write your own lines to connect them.

Robin Alvarez's first-and-last-line method: Make two lines by zig-zag selection. Use them as the first and last line of the poem, and write middle lines to connect them.

Myrna Folker's couplet method: Make the first line by zigzag selection. Write your own second line. Repeat for each couplet.

Sharon Pilling's triplet method: Make the first two lines by zigzag selection. Write your own third line. Repeat for each triplet.

Vito Belardinelli's quatrain method: Pick a row. Make four lines by square selection.

Jan Blankenberg's quatrain method: Pick a row. Make four lines, one line per square, by a modified version of square selection: use only the top and bottom words from each square and a word of your own to connect them.

Brenda Danker's quatrain method: Pick a row. Make one line per square by modified square selection: use only one word from each square and your own words.

Eliza Swafford's Poetry Checkers Rules: "King Points"

1) Players must make sentences using only the horizontal words that face them, one word from each row. The board may be moved to any side, but one side is used for one complete turn. Record sentences on separate paper.

2) If an acceptable sentence is made, the player wins ten king points. Sentences that have fewer than eight words win one king point per word.

3) Each time a sentence is made, the words used in it are then eliminated.

4) The players alternate turns until one player is stumped. The player with the most king points wins.

5) When the game is completed, the students write poems around an assigned number of sentences from the game.

Examples

To write the poem below, Charlene Engstrom used the board with the top row oriented as in the illustration. She described her method: "Starting at the top left of the Poetry Checkerboard, I chose one word from each box horizontally in the first row to make the first line. The second line is made up of my own words. The third line comes from the third line of boxes using the words in order across the row as per line one. Fourth line original. Fifth line again from checkerboard (using same method). Sixth, original. Seventh from checkerboard. And the last two lines, my own words."

> It's her snowy pies
> Of cold vanilla custard filled that
> Milky leaves grim flash
> Across my chilly teeth.
> At their neon undersides
> My chilled choppers chatter.

Around the warm train of
Chocolate syrup, crisp cherries do tumble.
Yummy! What a sweet trip!

Judy Slobodnick described her approach: "I chose a horizontal line and made sentences in each box, then put these sentences together with other sentences of my own to make the poem."

As my fruit pies cool on the counter,
I remember Penny's death.
That snowy night when your teardrops echoed
Each howl, filled with wrenching labor pains.
The barn so near that my body felt each pain, too.
Penny's daughter brings such joy to your playtime now,
As the shade of our home protects
      Your contentment
            As puppy and child sleep.

Becky Collins suggested that the Checkerboard user "pick two boxes randomly. Use as first and last lines. Fill in between to connect." Here is one of her examples:

I cool my pies.
You may drink plum wine wildly.
The plants grow well in hot weather.
My friend will pay for the damaged fender.

Myrna Folker started her lines from the squares containing the question words (*will, may, did, can*). The second line of each couplet is her answer. She "zigzagged down using a word from each box to get the first line of each stanza."

Ghost Chasing
(a question-answer game)

May she climb neon hills above her city?
Only if she takes her psychedelic kitty.

Will I dodge night ghosts near this house?
Perhaps, if I scare them with my white mouse.

Did you see wet cats in his hair?
I was running so fast I really didn't care!

Can you hang oak stars in that fence?
Sorry, I'm too tired, I've collapsed on this bench!

Robin Alvarez used "checker moves diagonally for the first and last lines" and wrote the middle lines to connect them.

They plant vines and chase leaves in the shade
As the spring rain bends and sways the willow branches they shelter
    under.
They lie side by side, holding hands laughing when the drops blind them
Giggling as they slide on the wet grass
Sighing when the time ends.

Returning images in the lonely dark—
Can you see wet lights in his hair?

Sharon Pilling's poem combined pairs of lines whose paths crossed on the Checkerboard. She "chose words going zigzag down the board wherever I chose, using one word per box."

Her heart beats slowly on red hot days.
Your heart beats slowly past red hot stars!

Alone their hearts beat.

My friend flashed wildly under crystal stars.
I will flash only on red hot days.

Alone we flash.

Brenda Danker "used one word from the top of a red square in a line going from left to right across the Checkerboard." The adverbs in each line came from the row she chose.

The neon flashed wildly
as I walked slowly
on my only trip
up the brightly lit strip.

Vito Belardinelli used words without changing their grammatical form, and he decided that the adverb *brightly* should stay that way in the second line. His brief description of his method: "Four words per square—in a row."

See, this flying saucer was spotted in Alaska
So we chased her brightly lights to Iowa.
Pete's mighty Texas muscles looked like Tree Vines
But his days are numbered
Because they now live in Utah.

Jan Blankenberg calls her approach the "single square top/bottom half square method." She used the checkerboard with the bottom row turned to the top. Going across that row (*you, I, we, they*), she placed *see* between two words in each square.

You see trees.
I see vases.
We see stars.
They see days.

CHAPTER 6

PUZZLE POETRY

Talk of mysteries!

—Henry David Thoreau, "The Maine Woods"

PUZZLE POETRY uses the format of a puzzle to pique students' curiosity. Writing the poem becomes a part of solving the puzzle, and vice versa. In each activity, the rules are simple and direct, and the goals are clear. Finding the solution offers a challenge that everyone can interpret in his or her own way.

In the Language Mazes, each student's solution forms a poem. In the Blank Puzzle Pieces and the Cardboard Star Puzzle, the words go together to make a larger poetry object, a jigsaw puzzle. In the Popsicle Puzzles, the lines of one student's poem become pieces of a puzzle for another student. And in Alphaboxes, the solution provides words to put in a poem.

Except for crossword puzzles, word search puzzles, and a few other kinds, most puzzles don't include words as part of the challenge. Yet combining words with non-verbal puzzles offers many ways to see how language works. For instance, the Haiku Maze shows how word choice affects meaning.

In fact, Coleridge wrote that "poetry = the best words in their best order." This suggests that a perfect poem is like a jigsaw puzzle: each word is a piece with its own place, and no other piece fits as well.

85. LANGUAGE MAZES

Ancient Greek mythology tells of the most famous maze in Western culture, the Minotaur's labyrinth that the master architect Daedalus designed. So complex was it that the hapless soul trapped inside had little chance of getting out. In modern times, Jorge Luis Borges explored the myth of the maze in *Labyrinths*, his collection of short stories about alternate realities.

In many ways, the maze is symbolic of life, which confuses with its labyrinthine choices. For children, however, the paper-and-pencil maze is a source of fun—challenging but not threatening. Every maze of this kind has at least one way out. Language, too, is a maze, and learning it can be just as confusing as Daedalus's labyrinth. Or it can be just as enjoyable as a paper-and-pencil maze. In Language Mazes, the student goes through the paths not with a straight line but with a poetic line.

Description

The students work the mazes according to the directions that follow. An option is to have students write longer poems based on what they read or write in the maze.

Highway Maze (see figure): Write words on the path till reaching the end. Try to pass as many words as possible and include them in the writing. (Best solution: Now-honk-curb-turn-slow-in-bump-highway-park.)

Yard Maze (see figure): Same directions as for Highway Maze. (Best solution: drool-bark-popcorn-cat-mutt-furry-banana-flea-moon-yum.)

Word Maze (see figure): Find the path that has complete and correct sentences from start to finish. (Solution: "The Word Maze twists and turns in the darkness, while I twist and turn at every word. Footsteps follow me. Shadows fool me. I try to speak, but my heart is pounding louder than words. What is that eerie light? It's the way out.")

Haiku Maze (see figure): Draw a line from start to finish. Circle one of the words in each word balloon along the way. No matter which path you take, the result is a seventeen-syllable haiku.

In all four mazes, two moves are forbidden: going back over a path already taken, and jumping over any lines or barriers that separate paths.

Materials

photocopy machine
Language Mazes (see figures)
pencils
writing paper

Preparation

Photocopy the maze(s) you plan on using.

Alternative

White out the words in the mazes, photocopy them, and ask your students to provide new words.

Examples

Below are two extreme solutions to the haiku maze. One sounds like a real haiku, and the other a surreal haiku. The words come from the same set of word balloons.

This glistening star
launches my boat: each evening

Highway Maze

Ringo Phone is driving to Electric City. He wants to take a route with a lot of signs on it. Show him how you would go by writing a poem through the maze. As you come to each sign, put the word on it in your poem.

Uara Mazze

Digit the Dog is really hungry! How many bones can she sniff out as she races through the yard? Help her by writing a poem through the maze to her doghouse. As you pass each bone, use the word on it in your poem.

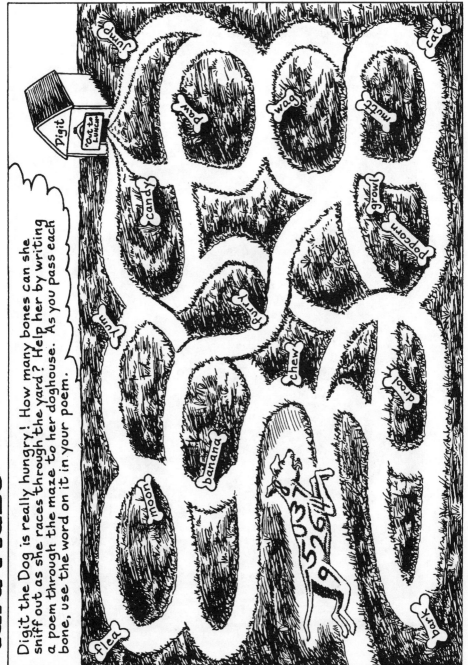

The Word Maze

Only one path makes sentences all the way to the end. Can you find it?

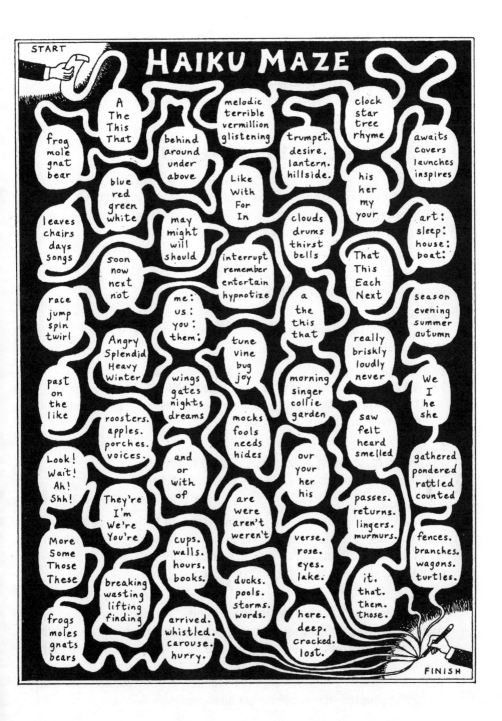

We counted branches.

A vermillion clock
covers my sleep: next summer
I rattled turtles.

86. BLANK PUZZLE PIECES

This activity is sure to puzzle the students—in a pleasant way. Even though they know what they've written, they don't know what the whole poem looks like on the "page." Which end is up? When they put the puzzle together, the words go in different directions.

Description
Each student writes words, phrases, and sentences on the pieces of a blank puzzle, and then assembles it.

Materials
blank puzzles (available through school supply stores)
colored felt-tip pens

Suggested Topics
1) "What is something that puzzles you about life?"
2) "If your words automatically made a picture when the puzzle was put together, what would the picture be?"

Suggestions
1) Glue the assembled puzzle to cardboard for display.
2) Take it apart and store it in a box for later assembly.

Alternative
Collaboration Puzzles: A few students write on their pieces and mix them together in a pile. Since the puzzles have the same cut-out pattern, the pieces are interchangeable. The students dig into the pile and assemble puzzles with pieces by everyone in the group.

Example
The students in my first Alternative Poetry Writing Class made a slightly different collaboration puzzle (see figure). Each student wrote phrases and lines on one or two pieces of a single blank puzzle and then assembled it. The Puzzle Pieces are by Arlet Anderson, Barb Edler, Valerie Kreutner, Linda Kruse, Lori Mueller, Sonia Wagner, Barbara Evans, Marcia Lohmann, Bobbette Lauer, and me.

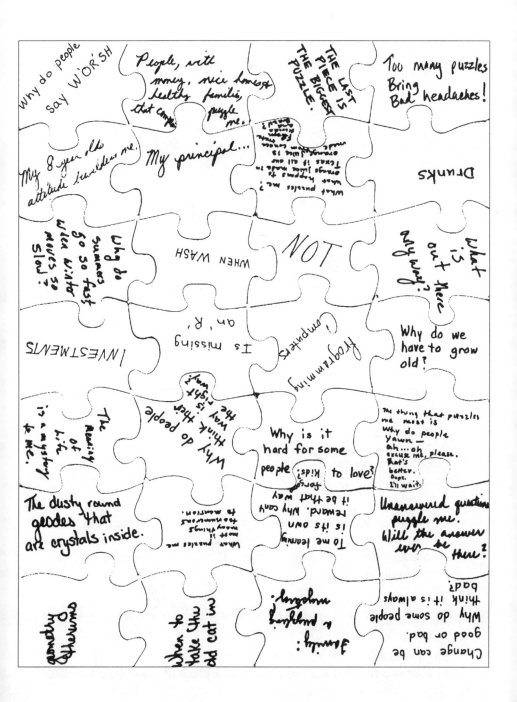

87. CARDBOARD STAR

In this puzzle, the pieces fit together to make a larger shape, but what is it? The students have an extra incentive to write—to find the answer to that question.

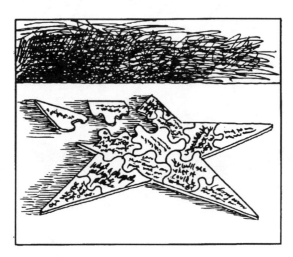

Description
The students write words, phrases, and lines on puzzle pieces and assemble them into a single large puzzle, a collaboration made up of individual fragments.

Materials
thick posterboard (24" x 36")
black felt-tip pens
scissors

Preparation
Draw a large star covering most of the posterboard and cut it out. Draw curving lines horizontally and vertically to divide the star up into puzzle pieces. Cut the star apart on the lines. Hand out one piece to each student without revealing the puzzle shape.

Suggested Topic
"What shape will the puzzle be when it's assembled? What does your puzzle piece look like? How might it fit in with the other pieces?"

Suggestions
1) Glue the finished Cardboard Star to a piece of posterboard for display.
2) Or take it apart and store it in a puzzle box.

1) Tell the students that the shape is a star, and ask them to write about stars.
2) Use several star puzzles made with different colors of posterboard and shuffle the pieces together. Give each student two or more differently colored pieces. The colors make it easy to separate the pieces and assemble the stars.
3) Cut out puzzles of different shapes (star, square, face, bird, etc.) Reveal the shapes to the students, and ask them to guess which shape their pieces came from.

Examples
(When I used this with the older people's poetry class, I told them the shape beforehand, and they wrote about it. Introductory questions included: "Do you remember any night when the stars looked especially dazzling in the sky? How did it affect you?")

> Going home from the skating rink
> At midnight, way north in Saskatchewan.
> We looked at the stars, especially bright.
> It was a sign of a change in the weather.
> The atmosphere in the north is lighter.
> The next day the change arrived.
> "Wow!"
>
> —*Nellie Voelkers, PCPO-Sixty*

> One late summer night
> Far to the south was a star
> Much larger and brighter
> Than all the others by far.
> The light of a huge steamer
> Surrounded by small boats
> All coming into port.
>
> —*Nellie Voelckers, PCPO-Sixty*

> Sitting on a blanket underneath the stars.
> My sweetie by my side.
> My hand and his tightly intertwined.
> We gazed up at the stars.
> We saw the Pleiades.
> The many twinkling stars
> Filled us with awe, with joy.
>
> —*Alice Gratke, PCPO-Sixty*

When love's arrow comes darting
like a star
through the sky
and pierces a lonely heart,
it goes flying on & on
into the sweet bye & bye.

—*Gladys Edwards, PCPO-Sixty*

Only once have I slept out under the stars.
'Twas in Gold Hill, Colorado.
In an old mining camp.
When I was young, imaginative and romantic.
The wind was
soughing through
the tall pines.
The air was
cold,
cold,
cold.

—*Alice Gratke, PCPO-Sixty*

88. POPSICLE PUZZLES

One student's poem is another student's puzzle. In this case, the second student tries putting the poem back together.

Description
Each student arranges ten popsicle sticks in a rectangle and writes a poem on them, one line per stick. Then everyone exchanges sets of sticks and tries to arrange each other's set in the order of the original poem. The students can also collaborate on larger poems by arranging the sticks from two or more sets.

Materials
popsicle sticks
colored felt-tip pens

Suggested Topics
1) "You're eating a popsicle on a hot day. It starts to melt all over something of great value. What does it melt on? Who owns the popsicle-drenched object? How can you make up for what happened? What flavor is the popsicle?"

2) "Make up a new product with a name ending in -*sicle*. How would you advertise it?"

Suggestions

1) After writing on the sticks, the student can number them on the back, to make it easier to assemble the poem.

2) To end the activity, collect all the sticks, mix them together well, and assemble them randomly into a single long poem. Then read the poem, or part of it, aloud.

89. ALPHABOXES

Alphaboxes (see figure) slide around to form words where the sides connect. Until the puzzle is solved, the squares make nonsense words at some of the connections. In either case, the student can use both types of words in a poem.

Description

Each student rearranges nine Alphaboxes to make a 3" x 3" square that spells short words horizontally and vertically where the edges connect. After eight minutes or so, time's up. Everyone writes a poem that includes all the words, both real and made-up, appearing in the boxes, plus many other words to connect them.

Materials

Alphaboxes: Two Puzzles in One
photocopy machine
colored card stock
scissors
black felt-tip pens
writing paper

Preparation

Photocopy "Alphaboxes: Two Puzzles in One" on colored card stock. Cut out the nine squares indicated by the two arrows at the edges, and put together sets of differently colored squares. Save the remaining seven squares for students who want to try the advanced version.

Alternative

Create more 3" x 3" puzzles by selecting other sets of nine boxes out of the sixteen provided. Some may have solutions, some may not. You can make at least one different set for every person you'll ever meet.

Alphaboxes: Two Puzzles in One

The set of Alphaboxes makes two puzzles of different sizes. Puzzle #1 uses nine boxes, which are marked off by the two small arrows. When you arrange the boxes in the correct 3" x 3" square, the words: EAR FIND AS YOKE UP IRE appear across, and HAM BIN NUT MOTE KISS RIDE go down. There may be other solutions.

Puzzle #2 requires all sixteen boxes. It works the same way, but no one, to my knowledge, has solved it.

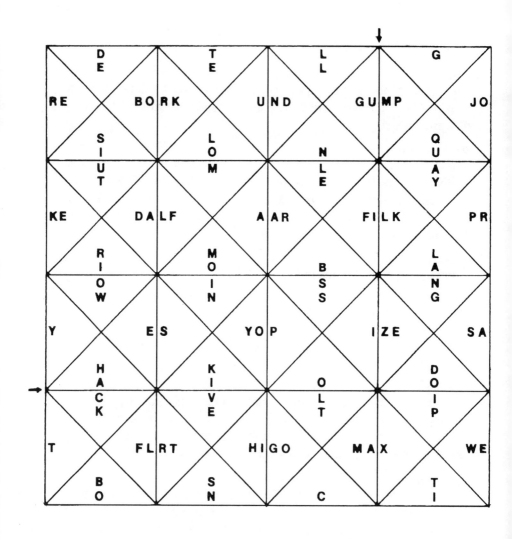

CHAPTER 7

AUTOMATIC POETRY

I dwell in Possibility—
A fairer House than Prose—

—Emily Dickinson, "657"

THE DEVICES in this chapter generate words, lines, or complete poems. While they work in different ways, they all rely on the chance juxtaposition of parts of speech. They resemble some of the puzzle poems, in that the words fit together to make a larger structure.

They work by the same principle as children's "flip-flop" books, which have the pages cut into three or so parts. By flipping to different combinations, the reader sees a new picture each time. Instead of pictures, automatic poetry devices have words chosen to fit together grammatically. The results don't usually make "normal" sense, but neither do the pictures in most flip-flop books. That is part of their appeal.

In some cases, such as Sliding Words, the students find words to put in their own poems. In other cases, such as Wonderverse, the poem writes itself.

90. WONDERVERSE

In making a poem, the poet selects one word out of many possibilities at each step. If all the alternatives were put together in every combination, the number of resulting poems would be incredibly large. Wonderverse demonstrates this phenomenon.

The students select words at random from the Word Map by touching a pencil point to the map and then write them on the Poem Board. Since the Word Map holds ten words for each blank on the Poem Board, it's extremely unlikely that two people will ever make the same poem.

Description
The student touches his or her pencil point to the Word Map to select words for the Poem Board. The words (numbered) go in blanks that have the corresponding numbers. The result: an automatic poem that looks like it came straight from Wonderland.

WORD MAP

POEM BOARD

$\frac{}{18 *}$ $\frac{}{25}$ $\frac{}{11}$ $\frac{}{30}$ $\frac{}{6}$ $\frac{}{16}$,

$\frac{}{23 *}$ $\frac{}{20}$ $\frac{}{17}$ $\frac{}{12}$.

$\frac{}{14 *}$ $\frac{}{7}$ $\frac{}{2}$ $\frac{}{21}$ $\frac{}{24}$ $\frac{}{16}$.

"$\frac{}{15 *}$ $\frac{}{8}$, $\frac{}{26 *}$ $\frac{}{22}$ $\frac{}{12}$!"

$\frac{}{23 *}$ $\frac{}{2}$ $\frac{}{4}$ $\frac{}{13}$ $\frac{}{3}$ $\frac{}{1}$,

$\frac{}{28 *}$ $\frac{}{2}$ $\frac{}{5}$ $\frac{}{19}$ $\frac{}{10}$.

$\frac{}{29 *}$, $\frac{}{9 *}$, $\frac{}{27}$ $\frac{}{1}$

$\frac{}{21 *}$ $\frac{}{24}$ $\frac{}{25}$ $\frac{}{10}$.

Suggestion
To underline the randomness, have the students close their eyes when they touch the Word Map.

Materials
photocopy machine
Word Map (see figure)
Wonderverse Poem Board (see figure)
pencils

Preparation
Photocopy the Wonderverse Poem Board and the Word Map.

Suggestion
To emphasize the randomness, have the students close their eyes when they touch the Word Map.

Example

> That yellow joke is washing gnats,
>   As angels dimly sew.
> She crumpled mice along these brats.
>   Joyce purred, "You shouldn't throw!"
>
> Where rugs might grind while winging,
>   Five bears hit fourteen lumps.
> O, Boomerang, you're dinging
>   Beneath those happy bumps.

91. SOCIAL SECURITY POEM

You can change your name, but you can't change your Social Security number. You can apply for a second number, but it doesn't erase the first. It's the only constant in life. Some children get their cards soon after turning two years old. By elementary school, many have "the card" and the number. Students can use their numbers to fill out this poetic tax form.

Description
Each person circles the eight digits of their Social Security number (or any eight digits), one per column, to make a poem.

Materials
Computation of Social Security Poem (see figure)
photocopy machine
pencils

SCHEDULE SE
(Form 1040)
Department of the Treasury
Internal Revenue Service

Computation of Social Security Poem ◄ ◄ ◄

▶ Attach to Form 1040.

23

Name of self-employed person (as shown on social security card)

Social security number of
self-employed person ▶

Your social security number determines your own unique poem hidden in a
billion possible poems below. To find yours, just circle the nine digits of your
social security number, one digit per column. Begin with the A-column for
your first digit, and continue through I. The corresponding phrases, when read
in the order of their selection, form your nine-line 1981 Social Security Poem.
Not only is it free verse, it's tax-deductible!

A
1. As the wheels
2. When other planets
3. Because her acorns
4. Since your lips
5. While those mannikins
6. If these shadows
7. After his dogs
8. Although our trucks
9. Before both dancers
0. Until their faces

B
1. were sleeping on
2. are flying around
3. don't bother
4. laughed at
5. bounced off
6. march around
7. will stumble over
8. can't taste
9. might paint
0. won't speak to

C
1. the singer's mouth,
2. his antique television,
3. her grand piano player,
4. these sad sandwiches,
5. those beautiful blue teeth,
6. that mindless table,
7. this magic Buick,
8. their golden typewriters,
9. an optical illusion,
0. a missing link,

D
1. he tried to whistle
2. she slapped him
3. he saw a ghost
4. she always grinned
5. he chuckled once
6. she wished him luck
7. he just pushed buttons
8. she read minds
9. he never sneezed
0. she almost ate dinner

E
1. down the sink.
2. against their beliefs.
3. between two mirrors.
4. at the Crystal Café.
5. like her telephone.
6. with the devil's lighter.
7. across Kansas.
8. without starlight.
9. in his dream.
0. out of sheer desire.

F
1. Her modern poetry
2. His astral projection
3. These lightning bolts
4. Their bathtub gin
5. That parking ramp
6. Random numbers
7. Your gothic romance
8. Those laser beams
9. My green thumb
0. The space shuttle

G
1. awkwardly
2. silently
3. jealously
4. haphazardly
5. neatly
6. voraciously
7. pitifully
8. gleefully
9. frankly
0. longingly

H
1. frightened the gnomes
2. pulled the plug
3. stunned the barber
4. praised the clock
5. attracted the mice
6. troubled the professor
7. boiled the shapes
8. angered the ambassador
9. caught the butterfly
0. bewildered the muse

I
1. floating in my soup.
2. upholstering his lawn.
3. naming those plants.
4. watching like an elephant.
5. looking for Fred.
6. training her cat.
7. evicting the landlord.
8. burning your toast.
9. hiding in their cellar.
0. glowing like a lamp.

Preparation

Photocopy the Social Security Poem form (above).

Example

Social Security Poem No. 496-50-9126

Since your lips
might paint
that mindless table,
he chuckled once
out of sheer desire.

My green thumb
awkwardly
pulled the plug
training her cat.

92. SHAKESPEAREAN SONNET MAKER

The Shakespearean Sonnet Maker takes up where the Bard of Avon left off. Composed of seventy carefully chosen lines of Shakespeare, it can generate 61,036,625 new sonnets.

Selecting the lines was a balancing act between rhyme and reason. Out of Shakespeare's original 2,156 lines, I picked fourteen sets of ten lines that rhymed. When I tried a few test sonnets, however, they made awkward grammatical jumps from line to line. I pared the sets down to five lines apiece, and that solved the problem.

Description
The students use two phone numbers (or any fourteen digits) to select from lists of Shakespeare's lines to make a sonnet. (See Shakespearean Sonnet Maker below for the directions.)

Materials
photocopy machine
Shakespearean Sonnet Maker (see figure)
pencils

Example

Sonnet No. 25262946080936

By looking on thee in the living day,
O let me, true in love, but truly write,
That I might see what the old world could say
And moan th' expense of many a vanish'd sight.
I grant I never saw a goddess go;
Two loves I have of comfort and despair,
Yet so they mourn, becoming of their woe,
As those gold candles fix'd in heaven's air:
When I have seen such interchange of state,
Bound for the prize of all-too-precious you,
Such civil war is in my love and hate
And I by this will be a gainer too;
Her audit, though delay'd, answer'd must be,
If ten of thine ten times refigur'd thee.

Write two seven-digit phone numbers here:

_____   _____

The two phone numbers have a total of fourteen digits, and there are fourteen sets of Shakespeare's lines below. Each line has two digits in front of it.

Start with the first digit in the phone numbers, then go to the first set of lines, find the digit that matches the phone digit, and circle it. Go back to the phone numbers, take the second digit, and circle the matching digit in the second set of lines. Continue matching digits and circling them for all fourteen sets.

When you're finished, read all the lines after the circled digits in the order of their appearance. It's a Shakespearean sonnet.

The number after each line refers to the sonnet it came from. Hence, 13.11 means sonnet 13, line 11.

1.

0,5 Against the stormy gusts of winter's day (13.11)
1,6 To let base clouds o'ertake me in my way (34.03)
2,7 By looking on thee in the living day (43.10)
3,8 When I perhaps compounded am with clay (71.10)
4,9 Then if he thrive and I be cast away (30.13)

2.

0,5 O let me, true in love, but truly write (21.09)
1,6 I tell the day, to please him, thou art bright (28.09)
2,7 Thy edge should blunter be than appetite (56.02)
3,8 Upon thy side against myself I'll fight (88.03)
4,9 I have seen roses damask'd, red and white (130.05)

3.

0,5 And fortify yourself in your decay (16.03)
1,6 And in mine own love's strength seem to decay (23.07)
2,7 That I might see what the old world could say (59.09)
3,8 And life no longer than thy love will stay (92.03)
4,9 For, thou betraying me, I do betray (151.05)

4.

0,5 And see the brave day sunk in hideous night (12.02)
1,6 And moan th' expense of many a vanish'd sight (30.08)

2,7 Yet doth it steal sweet hours from love's delight (36.08)
3,8 And sweets grown common lose their dear delight (102.12)
4,9 Which should transport me farthest from your sight (117.08)

5.

0,5 You had a father: let your son say so (13.14)
1,6 Toward thee I'll run, and give him leave to go (51.14)
2,7 I grant I never saw a goddess go (130.11)
3,8 What means the world to say it is not so (148.06)
4,9 Love's eye is not so true as all men's: no (148.08)

6.

0,5 Be not self-will'd, for thou art much too fair (6.13)
1,6 Against this coming end you should prepare (13.03)
2,7 In so profound abysm I throw all care (112.09)
3,8 And yet, by heaven, I think my love as rare (130.13)
4,9 Two loves have I of comfort and despair (144.01)

7.

0,5 Receiving [naught] by elements so slow (44.13)
1,6 If some suspect of ill mask'd not thy show (70.13)
2,7 That you yourself, being extant, well might show (83.06)
3,8 To give full growth to that which still doth grow (115.14)
4,9 Yet so they mourn, becoming of their woe (127.13)

8.

0,5 When your sweet issue your sweet form should bear (13.08)
1,6 As those gold candles fix'd in heaven's air (21.12)
2,7 Making his style admired everywhere (84.12)
3,8 And buds of marjoram had stol'n thy hair (99.07)
4,9 If Time have any wrinkle graven there (100.10)

9.

0,5 When I have seen such interchange of state (64.09)
1,6 If my dear love were but the child of state (124.01)
2,7 O'er whom [thy] gingers walk with gentle gait (128.11)
3,8 Past reasons hated, as a swallow'd bait (129.07)
4,9 With others thou shouldst not abhor my state (150.12)

10.

0,5 Whilst I, my sovereign, watch the clock for you (57.06)
1,6 Without all ornament, itself and true (68.10)
2,7 O, know, sweet love, I always write of you (76.09)
3,8 Bound for the prize of all-too-precious you (86.02)
4,9 Incapable of more, replete with you (113.13)

11.

0,5 Such civil war is in my love and hate (35.12)

1,6 Ruin hath taught me thus to ruminate (64.11)

2,7 For thee against myself I'll vow debate (89.13)

3,8 Thus policy in love, t'anticipate (118.09)

4,9 Love is my sin, and thy dear virtue hate (142.01)

12.

0,5 And you in Grecian tires are painted new (53.08)

1,6 Robbing no old to dress his beauty new (68.12)

2,7 Which should example where your equal grew (84.04)

3,8 Making their tomb the womb wherein they grew (86.04)

4,9 And I by this will be a gainer too (88.09)

13.

0,5 So thou through windows of thine age shall see (3.11)

1,6 Let this sad int'rim like the oceans be (56.09)

2,7 Let not my love be call'd idolatry (105.01)

3,8 Her audit, though delay'd, answer'd must be (126.11)

4,9 He is contented thy poor drudge to be (151.11)

14.

0,5 And, being frank, she lends to those are free (4.04)

1,6 If ten of thine ten times refigur'd thee (6.10)

2,7 Which in thy breast doth live, as thine in me (22.07)

3,8 Without accusing you of injury (58.08)

4,9 Whom thine eyes woo as mine importune thee (142.10)

93. DOLLAR BILL LIMERICK

When Edward Lear published limericks in his *Book of Nonsense,* he didn't realize how popular the form would become. It's probably the most widely-known poetic form in the English-speaking world. Like many other people, students enjoy its bouncy rhythm and rhyme.

In the Dollar Bill Limerick, the serial number on a dollar bill (or any eight-digit number) determines some of the words. As poet Wallace Stevens wrote, "Poetry is a kind of money."

Description

The students use a dollar bill serial number (or any eight-digit number) to select word lists and write them in the blanks on the Limerick Dollar (see figure) to make a limerick. See Limerick Word Lists (below) for the directions.

Instead of using the word lists, some students might prefer trying to complete the limerick with their own words.

Materials
dollar bill (or an eight-digit number)
photocopy machine
Limerick Dollar (see figure)
Limerick Word Lists (see figure)
black felt-tip pens

Preparation
Photocopy the Limerick Dollar and the Limerick Word Lists.

Suggestion
Bring some of Lear's limericks and illustrations for preliminary discussion. Point out the way Lear repeats, or almost repeats, the first line in the last line. Most other limericks use a different last line. Why did he do this?

Example

Dollar Bill Limerick No. 60641885

A raging young duck from the sky
Said, "I bought what a dollar can buy:
A flat belly tree
With a laughable key
And for dinner a soggy prune pie!"

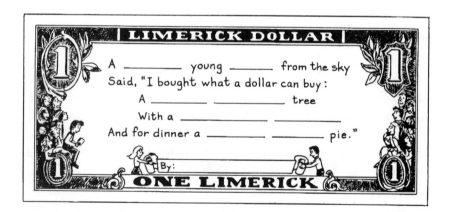

Write your serial number here: __ __ __ __ __ __ __ __

Now circle the numbers in these eight columns to select words, and write those words in the blanks on the Limerick Dollar. Put them in the same order as they appear here.

(1)	(2)	(3)	(4)
0 pretty	0 horse	0 blunt	0 penguin
1 corny	1 toad	1 lost	1 thimble
2 troubled	2 mole	2 sad	2 corkscrew
3 breathless	3 bat	3 trick	3 belly
4 woeful	4 ox	4 warped	4 ogre
5 raging	5 flea	5 flat	5 music
6 stingy	6 ant	6 rude	6 blackboard
7 hairy	7 pig	7 vile	7 widget
8 lively	8 sheep	8 true	8 yahoo
9 handsome	9 duck	9 wild	9 knicknack

(5)	(6)	(7)	(8)
0 jocular	0 flea	0 smelly	0 nut
1 mountainous	1 bee	1 queasy	1 cheese
2 horrified	2 knee	2 waxy	2 salt
3 virtual	3 pea	3 sticky	3 fish
4 runcible	4 tea	4 rubber	4 prune
5 tenderized	5 sea	5 pallid	5 grease
6 quizzical	6 fee	6 soggy	6 bean
7 downtrodden	7 key	7 knobby	7 stew
8 limerick	8 plea	8 clammy	8 clam
9 portable	9 ski	9 moldy	9 ham

94. THE WORD BOARD

The Word Board is a simple device for generating sentences. At first I wasn't certain that it would offer enough possibilities or that it would have the appeal of a more complex device. However, when I tried it with the Poetry Class for People over Sixty, the students liked how it looked and appreciated its simplicity.

The original Word Board was limited to three-word sentences. This new version makes sentences of any length, thanks to the addition of prepositions in each of the corners.

WORD BOARD

by	dime	mouse	waffle	jelly	ant	needle	town	lemon	ivy	pool	for
orange	woke	earns	itched	fills	clipped	gets	made	bends	juggled	rubs	eagle
car	aims	knew	visits	created	tricks	broke	quotes	nudged	unveils	fixed	island
mail	grazed	dents	zapped	ropes	loved	empties	opened	yokes	peeled	annoys	starch
color	invents	baked	upsets	asked	votes	dug	stops	had	lacks	touched	window
fudge	needed	coaxes	quit	takes	won	paints	gulped	doubts	spilled	knits	bath
gold	x-rays	nabbed	jilts	fought	bugs	ironed	pushes	okayed	misses	viewed	ring
paper	sold	moves	caught	haunts	quilted	zips	ate	slaps	united	bites	hose
lion	uses	ended	dusts	yelled	oozes	added	melts	planted	tastes	joined	face
elm	kicked	helps	queried	loses	valued	ignores	raked	yanks	xeroxed	fans	odor
vase	owns	wore	rolls	kept	jumps	yielded	gyps	named	wears	lit	zero
with	bike	arm	goat	toy	quest	door	news	year	key	umbrella	to

The student makes a sentence by pointing to any noun square on the perimeter and moving any number of squares horizontally, vertically, or diagonally to stop on another square. Then he or she writes a poem with the sentence as its title.

The squares contain different kinds of words: corner squares have prepositions, edge squares have nouns, and center squares have transitive verbs. Nouns have to begin sentences, end sentences, and end prepositional phrases. Verbs connect nouns as subjects and direct objects. Prepositions lead into nouns. (It's OK for students to add articles and conjunctions of their own.)

Materials
photocopy machine
Word Board (see figure)
black felt-tip pens
writing paper

Preparation
Photocopy the Word Board (and enlarge if necessary).

Suggestions
1) Instead of the moves described above, the student picks any word from its appropriate area.
2) Glue the "Word Board" illustration to a piece of wood to make it more durable.
3) Try a different way of selecting the words, such as flipping coins onto the board until two nouns and a verb are hit.
4) Replace the words with words of your own.

Alternative
Sharon Pilling's multi-line method: make several three-word lines, and include a few words of your own (see below).

Examples

Lemon Doubt Iced

Don't ever doubt
that your Iced
Lemon Tea
will ever be
anything
but tasty.

—*Gladys Edwards, PCPO-Sixty*

Gold Jams Toy

Gold is found
in rock jams in Alaska, as
the toy shovels go to work

    —Clarice Stenby, PCPO-Sixty

Jelly Asks Window

The jelly sits in the window
shining in the sun
It settles and shakes with laughter
and asks what it should have done—

The window asks the jelly
Why do you sit on my shelf?
To stiffen and shine he answered
and satisfy myself

    —Pearl Minor, PCPO-Sixty

Poker Wakes Boy

The alarm failed to rouse the boy,
So the poker stirring the fire
Said, I bet he wakes up
When I get the fire started.

    —Myldred Strong, PCPO-Sixty

Sharon Pilling, in my Alternative Poetry Writing Methods class, took a different approach. She made several three-word sentences with the board. In a few instances, she used her own words instead (*My, Little, Damsel, gets, Dad, Mom, lip*) to give more meaning to the following funny vignette:

My Little Knight

Toy visits jelly.
Bike dusts ant.
Car dents elm.
Knight jumps town.
Mail paints news.
Damsel gets ring.
Dad pushes door.
Mom bites lip.

    —Sharon Pilling

95. SLIDING WORD STRIPS

Sliding Word Strips offer another way to generate sentences. They're easy to make and easy to use. When you slide them together to make one sentence, other sentences appear in all the other lines.

Making the strips was tricky. At first I placed words randomly in the grid, but when I cut the strips out for a test run, they didn't make very many sentences. So I tried selecting words that, like those on the Word Beads (below), could substitute for each other in a global sentence. This approach worked better, but the strips were still restricted to a specific order. To give them more flexibility, I picked words that are both nouns and verbs to put in the second and third columns.

As well as generating ideas for poetry, the strips demonstrate sentence formation.

Description

The student lays the Sliding Word Strips next to each other, moves them around, and slides them up and down to make sentences. Then he or she writes a poem with the sentences.

Here are some suggestions for using different numbers of sentences in poems:

One sentence—Use it as the first line of a rhyming couplet, and write the second line.

Two sentences—Write one sentence at the top of the page and one at the bottom. Write lines in between to connect them.

Three sentences—Use each sentence to begin a different stanza of a three-stanza poem.

Four sentences—Write the sentences double-spaced. Then write lines between the sentences to connect them.

Any number of sentences—Put the sentences together to make a poem without writing any new lines.

Materials

photocopy machine
Sliding Word Strips (see figure)
colored cardstock
scissors
envelopes
black felt-tip pens
writing paper

Preparation

Photocopy the strips onto a variety of colors of cardstock paper. Cut them out in columns as indicated by the small arrows. Then make

your	secret	faces	name	those	words	on	paper
which	hungry	kids	taste	the	pies	before	lunch
the	noisy	fans	cheer	her	dreams	of	baseball
their	glowing	fires	heat	few	tents	in	time
his	haunted	houses	fear	most	ghosts	until	dawn
her	hidden	alarms	watch	some	clocks	through	glass
what	tiny	drops	splash	his	elms	with	rain
the	clever	tricks	fool	many	wizards	by	magic
no	broken	mirrors	doubt	your	eyes	about	beauty
our	earthy	plants	water	such	roots	at	night
the	neon	lights	show	more	stars	after	dark
your	musical	notes	help	all	tunes	beyond	belief
my	quick	changes	turn	the	minutes	to	dust
its	rumbling	clouds	cover	our	houses	for	winter
the	final	acts	play	these	scenes	from	memory

sets of the same color and sets of different colors. Place each set in an envelope.

96. WORD BEADS

One Christmas several years ago, I gave strings of Word Beads as gifts. The recipients enjoyed getting something that didn't come mass-produced for the holiday season.

The students can also make their own portable poetry generators out of macramé beads. The beads rotate on the string to form different surrealistic lines of poetry. It's fun to watch.

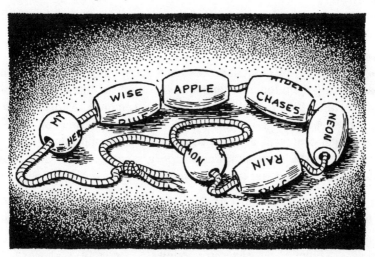

Description
The students write a sentence of five or six words across the page. Then they write sets of alternative words under each word. These words should work equally well in the sentence. Then the students write or print each set of words around a macramé bead and string all the beads together.

Materials
scissors
macramé string
macramé beads
black felt-tip pens
writing paper

1) Try having the students write longer sentences to put on more beads.
2) They can make "punctuation beads" with four different punctuation marks—period, question mark, exclamation point, and ellipsis—encircling them to end their moveable sentences.
3) Display the strings of beads on rectangular boards. Hang several strings in parallel rows like the lines of poetry on a page.
4) Put several students' beads on a single long string. Each set should end with a blank bead or a punctuation bead to separate it from the set that comes after it. Display the beads by hanging the string across the room.

Alternative
After stringing the beads, the students rotate them to find ideas, titles, and first lines for poems.

Sample Word Bead List
The six lists below contain words for macramé beads. Write them on beads, string them together, and spin them around like the wheels of a slot machine. Every combination makes a sentence. Altogether, there are 4 x 4 x 4 x 4 x 4 x 4 = 4,096 possible six-word sentences.

Longer sentences are easy to make. For example, inserting a column of adverbs such as *quickly, softly, neatly, dimly,* and *grossly* between the second and third columns makes a seven-word sentence.

1st bead	*2nd bead*	*3rd bead*	*4th bead*	*5th bead*	*6th bead*
Pronoun	**Adjective**	**Noun**	**Verb**	**Adjective**	**Plural noun**
My	wise	apple	chases	neon	rain
Her	blue	shadow	views	greedy	horns
His	mad	face	ignores	tender	dawn
Your	young	parrot	hides	lumpy	jars

97. TRAIN OF THOUGHT

Children enjoy construction kits, like Lego and Lincoln Logs, because of the challenge of building big things out of small pieces. This exercise consists of a kit for building sentences out of words. All connections work no matter how the student arranges them (see figures).

Description
The student arranges any number of Word Tracks with their ends touching so as to make a pattern of sentences. Then he or she builds outward with Blank Tracks and writes words on them to make sentences branching out at the connections. After using five or more

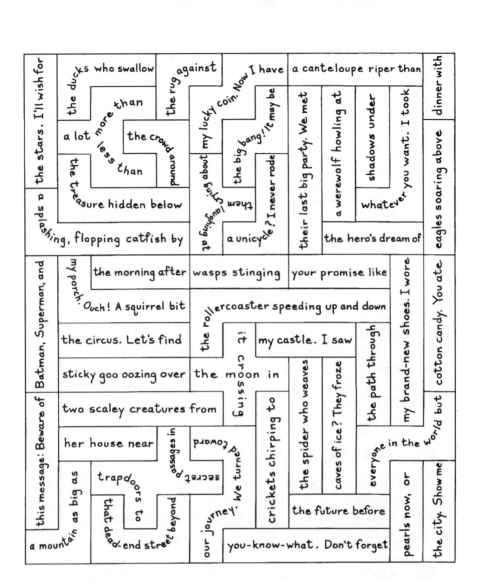

Blank Tracks, the student writes a poem on paper. The poem should include some or all of the words written on the tracks, as well as other words to complete it.

Materials

photocopy machine
Word Tracks (see figure)
Blank Tracks (see figure)
white or light-colored cardstock
scissors
pens
paper

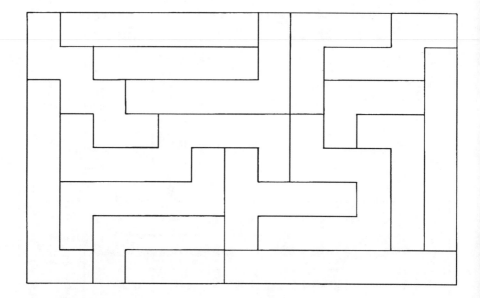

Preparation
Photocopy the Word Tracks and the Blank Tracks onto cardstock. Cut them out along the solid lines.

98. LETTER GALAXY

Look at the letters floating in a bowl of alphabet soup. Without too much searching, you'll find a few words. It's an automatic response. Any random array of letters will have clusters that form words, and any cluster of words can inspire a poem.

Description
The students look for words in the Letter Galaxy (see figure) and circle ten or more. They write poems that include those words and their own.

Materials
photocopy machine
colored paper
Letter Galaxy (see figure)
black felt-tip pens
writing paper

Preparation
Photocopy the Letter Galaxy on paper of different colors.

206

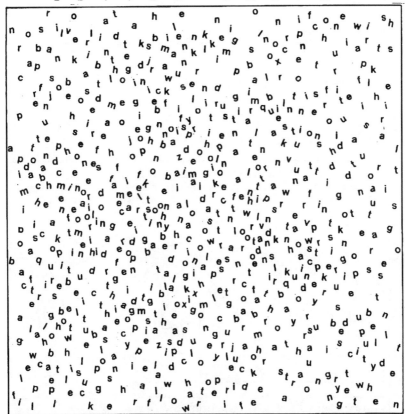

99. CARTOON CARDS

Any way you arrange them, the Cartoon Cards make a line of talking heads speaking in rhyming couplets. The couplets change with every arrangement of the cards.

Description

The students move the Cartoon Cards around to find a couplet they like. They write two or more lines to complete the poem. The lines can rhyme, but they don't have to.

Materials

photocopy machine
cardstock
Cartoon Cards (see figure)
black felt-tip pens
writing paper

Preparation
Photocopy the cards on cardstock and cut them out.

Alternatives
1) The student writes a rhyming couplet to complete one or more of the couplets on the cards.
2) The student writes a rhyming couplet that goes *before* the couplet on the cards.

100. ALPHABET MUSIC CODE

From Mother Goose to the Mothers of Invention, music has always been closely linked with rhyming poetry. Less has been done to connect music and unrhymed poetry, but poets have occasionally experimented with the combination. I've met a number of teachers who have had their students write poetry while listening to music.

In this activity, poetry actually turns into music. The code below provides a simple way to convert words, letter by letter, into a series of musical notes. The result: an amusing atonal tune.

Description
The students print poems of four to eight lines on music composition paper. Then the teacher or the students use the Alphabet Music Code to convert the letters to musical notes. (For directions, see How to Use the Alphabet Music Code below.) The teacher finds someone to play part of each work in person or on tape to be replayed in class.

Materials
photocopy machine
Alphabet Music Code (see figure)
music composition paper
black felt-tip pens
musical instrument
tape recorder

Preparation
Photocopy the Alphabet Music Code

Suggested Topics
1) "What is your favorite musical instrument? Why do you like it? Do you play it or know someone who does?"
2) "If you started your own band, what would you call it? Why?"
3) "Imagine you're somewhere in the country. You hear beautiful music in the distance. What are the surroundings? What time of day is it? What season? Think of the colors, the smells, and the sights. How does the music fit in with them?"

Suggestion
A more tonal code could be created by having all the letters stand for two harmonic notes in a row instead of one note. You may want to make up your own two-note code and use it.

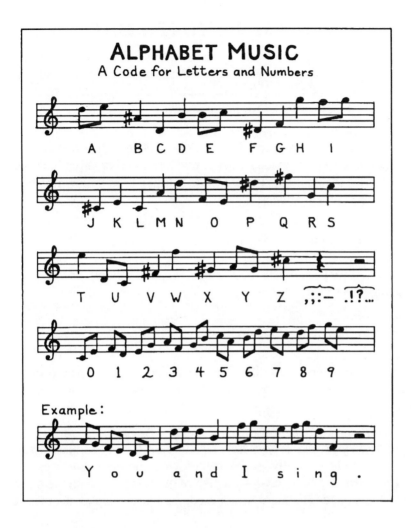

How to Use the Alphabet Music Code

Find the letter, number, or punctuation mark to be encoded, look for the musical equivalent (one or two notes) above it on the staff, and draw it on music composition paper. Repeat for all letters, numbers, and punctuation marks. If a symbol isn't musically coded, such as a quotation mark, exclude it.

The code isn't completely random. In designing it, I matched up the more commonly used letters with the natural notes, and the rarer letters with sharps and flats. Also, I picked some frequently used suffixes and words and encoded their letters to produce a melodic sequence of notes.

101. ALPHABET PICTURE CODE

The link between pictures and words is age-old, first appearing in the symbols painted on the walls of caves. Pictographic languages such as Chinese use pictures for words; the alphabet picture code goes in the other direction, making words into pictures.

Description
The students use the Alphabet Picture Code to change their first and last names into drawings made of geometric shapes. (For directions, see How to Use the Alphabet Picture Code below.) Then they write about what their drawings suggest.

Materials
photocopy machine
Alphabet Picture Code (see figure)
colored felt-tip pens (black, blue, green, red, and yellow)
drawing paper

Preparation
Photocopy the Alphabet Picture Code.

Suggested Topic
"What do the shapes look like? Do you see any objects? Any people? What are they doing? Where is this happening? Write a poem about the picture."

Alternatives
1) Students pick four words, draw a picture for each one on a separate page, and write a narrative poem about it with one stanza per page.
2) They write a poem and draw a picture of all the words in the poem on a single page. The more words used, the more complex the picture becomes.

Alphabet Picture Code

    A black straight line
    B blue curved line
    C green wavy line
    D red zigzag line
    E yellow circle
    F black triangle
    G blue square
    H green rectangle
    I red star
    J yellow straight line

K black curved line
L blue wavy line
M green zigzag line
N red circle
O yellow triangle
P black square
Q blue rectangle
R green star
S red straight line
T yellow curved line
U black wavy line
V blue zigzag line
W green circle
X red triangle
Y yellow square
Z black rectangle

How to Use the Alphabet Picture Code
Find the letter to be encoded and draw its color shape anywhere on the page. Choose the size and location of the shape. Repeat for all the letters. Since the size and the placement of the shapes are at the discretion of the student, no two pictures, even pictures of the same word, will look very much alike.

102. POETRY KALEIDOSCOPE

When you twist the end of this kaleidoscope, letters and words move around in the most amazing patterns! Of all the poetry devices, this one gives a view of language unlike any you've ever seen. It's concrete poetry in motion.

One evening I went to Goodwill with my five-year-old son to find some good used toys for him. While he rummaged through the Micro Machines, I picked up a kaleidoscope and looked through it. The usual, but somewhat faded, color patterns danced around. I wondered why I'd never seen *words* in kaleidoscopes instead. Maybe they wouldn't work very well. To find out, I bought the kaleidoscope.

At home, I popped out the plastic disc on the front, poured out the color pieces, and put in a few cut-out words. When I held the kaleidoscope up to the light, the image was disappointing. The paper made reading difficult. "So that's why they don't make them," I thought.

A few days later, however, I decided to take another approach. If words on paper didn't work, perhaps words on transparencies would. I went to the copy center and had a page of words copied on a clear sheet of acetate. At home, I cut out the words, put them in the kaleidoscope, and looked through it. Wow! I felt like I was looking at a new world of words. It worked better than I'd ever imagined it would.

Description
Students look through the Poetry Kaleidoscope and write poems about what they see.

Materials
kaleidoscope
pocket knife
tweezers
photocopy machine
scissors
Elmer's glue
white paper
transparent acetate sheet

Preparation
To make the kaleidoscope, carefully remove the plastic disc that covers the end containing the color pieces. To do this, cut a small hole or slit near the edge of the circle, insert tweezers, and pull the disc out. Dump out the pieces. Put in words of your choice, replace the disc, and tape it shut.

To prepare the words, cut them out from printed pages (or from your own typewritten sheets) and photocopy them at different sizes on regular paper. Cut out words of different sizes, glue them to a single sheet, and have that sheet photocopied on a transparent sheet of acetete. Cut out these words and use them in the kaleidoscope.

Suggestion
Try several different combinations of letters, words, typefaces, etc., until you come up with a combination you like. Using a small number of words (five or fewer results in simple, elegant patterns that sometimes repeat; a larger number of words increases the pattern possibilities; too many words makes an illegible chaos).

Alternative
Students write a short poem, and the teacher copies it onto a transparent page. Students cut up the copy, put some of the words in the kaleidoscope, and look at them.

Advice Poem

Wands are fun while babysitting!

*

While tap dancing you'll make a click, click, click.

*

Tablecloths are as boring as a spare tire.

—*Samantha Soll, sixth grade*

103. WORD CALCULATOR

The main character in Stanley Kubrick's science-fiction film *2001* is named Hal. That name has special significance. If you move one step down the alphabet for each letter in HAL, you get IBM (H to I, A to B, and L to M). HAL was an IBM computer.

HAL and IBM form what is called a lettershift pair. There are many other lettershift words, but most require moving more than one step down the alphabet. Finding them can be time-consuming. You have to write a word and then write the alphabet downward starting with each letter in the word. This column of words shows how CHEER eventually leads to JOLLY:

CHEER
DIFFS
EJGGT
FKHHU
GLIIV
HMJJW
INKKX
JOLLY

The Word Calculator (see figure) is a device that simplifies the search and makes it fun. For people who haven't heard about lettershift words, operating the Word Calculator provides a lot of surprises.

Students enjoy looking to see whether their names make lettershift words. When one of my students checked her last name, BERRY, she found ANN in another row. Incredibly, her name is ANNE BERRY (ANN is close enough). When I checked my last name, MORICE, the name GIL turned up. That was my father's name.

The Calculator can generate words for poems. Many lettershift pairs are quite poetic.

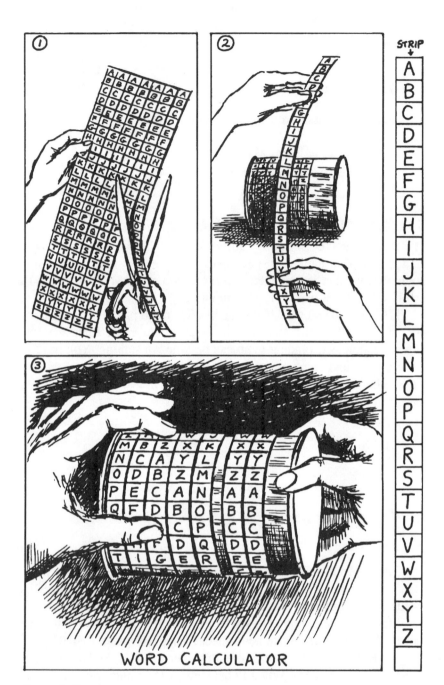

WORD CALCULATOR

Description

The student looks for lettershift words on the Word Calculator. The words don't have to be complete shifts, such as CHEER-JOLLY. Partial shifts can be just as inspiring. After finding a few, the student makes the lettershift words into a poem.

Materials
photocopy machine
Word Calculator (see figure)
can of soup (unopened)
scissors
black felt-tip pens
writing paper

Preparation
Copy the strip of letters seven or eight times from the Word Calculator figure. Wrap each strip around an unopened can of soup. Glue the A-square at the top of the strip over the blank square at the bottom.

Because the figure is smaller than the original, you will have to enlarge the copies, testing them on a can until you get the right size.

CHAPTER 8

STUDENT-MADE METHODS

Tattoo a poem on yourself.

—Kent Wilson

104. HOW WOULD YOU WRITE?

At the beginning of this book, I asked you to write the word *poetry* on an object. Now, before reading any further, try making up the most extreme poetry writing method you can imagine. You can write with anything, you can write on anything, and you can do it anywhere you want. Your method can be so extreme that it defies the laws of nature. You have no limits.

Description

The students come up with unusual ways to write poems. After brainstorming for a few minutes, they each describe their methods.

•

In 1976, I taught in my first Poetry-in-the-Schools residency. The program took place at Southdale Elementary School in Cedar Falls, Iowa. I conducted twenty one-hour workshops during the week-long program. About 195 students in grades four through six participated by attending three workshops each.

During that week, the students wrote poems using three different methods: Poetry Poker, Wooden Word Doors, and Paper Sky Writing. After creating their own poems during the week, they invented their own unusual methods of writing poetry, an assignment they tackled with enthusiasm and creativity.

> Write it on a mustache
> write it on a dog
> write it on the snow
> write it on an elephant tusk
> write it on some glasses
> write it on a fossil
> write it in a pumpkin

write it on a tree
write it on leaves

—Eddie Ihde

By taking a turnabout-is-fair-play approach, students have the opportunity to think about the mechanics of writing. I tell them they can come up with possible and impossible ways to write poetry. Some students favor one or the other. Most give examples at both extremes.

Write a poem on the bottom of your shoe
Use a bunch of melted crayons and a quill pen and write it on a piece of
    paper
Write a poem on a carpet
Go under water and write a poem on a piece of waterproof paper
Write a poem on your wall with markers or crayons or pencil or ink it
    doesn't matter
Cut off some of your hair and put it underneath a piece of paper nicely
    then write your poem on the paper and there will be pencil marks
    where the hair was or else string a thread or yarn it depends on what
    you want to use.

—Gia Wadle

Before the students write, I have them brainstorm for about five minutes. At that point, some start champing at the bit. They want to get their ideas down on paper, and they come up with new ideas as they write. One idea sparks the next one. The following student had to make up a word *thrillionth* to measure what must be the tiniest possible writing surface ever.

Write one down a dam while it's breaking up.
Write one under the Pacific Ocean.
Write one with fifty king cobras.
Write it on a great white shark.
Write it on a python
Write it on a grain of sand
Write it on a thrillionth of an atom
Write it on a train track
Write it on Mount Everest
Write it on a fern
Write it on a pencil
Write it on a firework
Write it on a horse's tail.

—Mike Allen

Many of the students' methods show great cleverness in combining words with objects. Given that the students hadn't thought about their own methods until a few minutes before writing, the ideas are that much more amazing.

Write a poem with flares
Go up to the moon and put a poem up on the moon.
Tap out a Morse Code poem with shotgun shells.
Paint a poem on a house.
Get scuba gear and go in the Bermuda Triangle.
Take a lot of people and get them in line so they spell a poem.

—*Steve Smalley*

Around the world
On a forty-dollar shirt
Put one in any fastest rocket
Write one on a dime and throw it off the Empire State Building

—*Mike Resvik*

One method caught me completely off guard. A fourth grade girl who looked a little like the Munsters' daughter had been quietly attentive all week. When I asked for poetry-writing ideas, she raised her hand. It was the first time she'd volunteered to speak. In a shy, quiet voice, she said, "You could write a poem on a dead body."

"Yes, that would be a different surface," I replied evenly. "What kind of pens would you use?" She said felt-tip markers might work best. A few students wanted to know how the person died.

Living creatures also come up in the students' methods. The first method below would get you arrested, and the last one would send you to the hospital.

Go to Hollywood, grab a famous movie star, take off his coat, and write a poem.

—*Debbie Bergeson*

Write a poem on a cow.

—*Kent Wilson*

If you have blonde hair, write on it.

—*Laurie Klages*

Write a poem on a bald man's head

—*Jennifer Brobst*

Write it closing your eyes
Write it on your forehead
Write it inside an alligator's mouth
Write it on a bucking strap—while it's on the horse!

—*Stephanie Carlson*

Write a poem on a feather of a bird

—*Harold Parker*

Write on Jimmy Carter's teeth, write in red, white and blue magic markers.

—*Anonymous*

Print one on the principal's face

—*Mike Resvik*

A clock that says a poem when it strikes the hour.

—*Anonymous*

Write it while standing on white hot coals in the dark

—*Harold Parker*

The wildest Rube Goldberg idea came from a student whose name I don't know. He described it during the brainstorming session, and it went something like this:

Two jet planes fly next to each other with a long piece of paper stretching from the wing of one plane to the wing of the other. Another jet plane flies above them with a swing hanging down close to the paper. Somebody sits on the swing and writes the poem while the planes keep flying.

Airplanes are popular poetry vehicles. Here are a few other high-flying methods:

Get an airplane and sky write

—*Sean Riley*

Paint a poem on a hot air balloon. Paint a poem on a parachute.

—*Todd Richard*

Write one when you skydive.

—Greg Starbeck

Go up in a plane and parachute down and write a poem when you're coming dowwwwwwwwn.

—Michael Poe

Occasionally, a student will come up with a method and others will say, "Wow! You could sell that." The idea of making a marketable poetry object isn't that far-fetched. If people enjoy Scrabble, Boggle, and other letter games, perhaps poetry games would work as well. The other day my five-year-old son overheard me discussing this book with a friend. He interrupted the conversation with an air of urgency and excitement in his voice.

"What is it, Danny?"

"I know something you could do. Poetry Legos. Put words on Legos and when you build something, it makes a poem."

And I didn't know he was aware of what I was writing about in this book!

Recently, I asked a group of fourth–eighth graders at a Young Writers' Conference in Mt. Pleasant, Iowa, to brainstorm ways to write poetry. One student came up with an original idea, and the others spun off it without hesitation.

First student: "You could build a city with the houses arranged to spell out the words of a poem you could read from an airplane."

Second student: "Then you could plant flowers in the shape of letters to spell out more poems so people could see them on the ground."

Third student: "And you could trim the hedges to make more poems."

Sometimes the methods become quite complex:

Make about an acre of cement and while it's still wet take shingles and make them into a short poem.

—Kristen Spande

Write a thousand poems and put them in a hot air balloon. Let the balloon go up in the air. Let it come down in a different colony.

—Theo Strable

Get a typewriter and then get in your car if you have one then go downtown and type a long poem and put it out the window.

—Greg Weigel

Write a poem at a football stadium.
Write one letter on every seat till you're done with the poem.

—*Leonard Duncan*

At what point do students feel they've gone too far? Judging from the methods above, there seem to be hardly any limits at all. However, one girl found a method she thought would bring an end to her career as a poet.

Writing a poem that's full of foam.
When Mom sees it she screams and moans and says don't write any
more poems!

—*Brett W.*

POETRY BY CHILDREN WITH SPEECH AND HEARING IMPAIRMENTS

Teaching at the Iowa School for the Deaf gave me a new view of the English language. I hadn't realized how deeply our concepts of grammar are affected by our learning to speak. Nor had I ever run across English that was structured so differently. The students wrote poems that expressed their ideas in ways that made language seem new and fresh to me.

In the spring of 1976, I participated in a forty-hour poetry writing program with 150 students from grades one through nine. Five classes met on Monday and Tuesday of each week. Since I didn't know sign language beyond finger-spelling, a counselor signed for me. The students were an extremely enthusiastic, high-energy group of children and teenagers. Outside of class, they didn't let my lack of knowledge of American Sign Language get in the way of talking with me. Small groups of students would sign to me as if I were one of them. Usually there was someone nearby, a student or counselor, who could tell me what they were saying.

One twelfth grade student, Anthony Greene, joined in the classes. He wanted to be a writer (and he was certainly talented). Only slightly hearing impaired, Tony spoke and signed English as fluently as people on either side of the sound barrier. Outside of class, he and I became friends united in our interest in writing. Sometimes we talked about language. He said that people who have been deaf for most of their lives think with little hands signing the words rather than a mental voice speaking them.

I learned a little signing, enough to notice ways that it differs from the way I speak and write. When signing, the speaker often omits articles, pronouns, prepositions, and the verb *is*. Past and future tenses are used less frequently. Adjectives can be used as nouns. As with many foreign languages, the predicate can come before the subject, and an adjective can follow the noun it modifies.

Tony said that he viewed signing as a different kind of spoken language. Through use, the signers have found the structures that work best for them. Each word in sign language requires more time and energy than a spoken word, and so linguistic evolution takes its course: language follows a direct path toward meaning.

To involve all the students, I decided to use activities that allowed for a wide spectrum of interpretations. For one activity, students made up lists of things about themselves. In another, they wrote about an animal by beginning each sentence with the animal's name. In a third activity, they wrote about a poster-sized drawing of a cosmic Cheshire Cat with teeth made of American flags, a tail that wrapped around the world, and other bits of surrealism.

I also used Poetry Poker, but the regular rules must have been interpreted differently by the counselor and the students. Instead of using all the words on the cards, the students picked only those words that they wanted to use and wrote them in paragraph form. The results were great—some of my favorite works!

Working with them was different from working with hearing students. Because I had to give directions through the counselor, it took a little longer to establish the trust and rapport so necessary in a writing class. Other than that, they worked as hard as any group to make their poems, and when they finished they brought them up to me for my reaction. I responded as much as I could through hand and facial gestures, and made spoken comments that the counselor conveyed on the spot.

When I read what they wrote, I was amazed at how expressively many of them used written English. I tried to imagine how it would be to learn letters, words, and sentences without ever hearing them. Their sentence structures differed at times from the structures I'm accustomed to, but those differences result from the students' quite logical approach to English.

Their word-list poems showed how the way language is learned affects the way it is spoken and written. The students learned written English by what Tony called "the apple tree method." It relies on sets of sentences having the same structure, and it leaves some words out for the student to try alternative words, a kind of fill-in-the-blank approach. But this doesn't always work in proper English.

The students' "incorrect" but logical use of English resulted in some wonderful lines of poetry. How can one improve on the precision and simplicity of "The tree is apple" by Tina Jarvis? To me it's much more interesting than "It is an apple tree."

At the end of the poetry program, I published a class magazine, *Rubber Band*, presenting one poem by each student. When I passed out the magazine, the students were quite eager to look at it. Many of them read it all the way through on the spot.

These poems can broaden the language experience of hearing students as well. The teacher can read some of the poems and discuss the grammar. Can the students restate the ideas in mainstream English?

How does such a rewrite alter the meaning and impact of the original? The unfamiliar grammatical structures can lead into a discussion of foreign languages that follow different rules than those of English.

The teacher can also ask the students to write their own poems using nonstandard structures, such as putting all the verbs at the beginning of the sentences or using adjectives as if they were nouns. Each student can make up one or two rules to follow in writing the poem. Afterwards, when the poems are read aloud, the other students can try to figure out the rules.

As adults, we take language for granted. We think we have mastered it, but it's really mastered us. We form sentences according to deceptively strict rules and routines. Poems such as these by students with impaired hearing show us fresh ways to stretch the language and to do something beautiful with it.

Poems from Rubber Band

My Favorite Music

I like to play guitar.
And I play piano.

And my favor is flower.

I like to smell flower.
And see how is pretty flower.
And different kinds of flower.
Purple or yellow, anything.

And my favor is tree.
I like to see what kinds
of tree. They had leaves.
And I had at my home
is oak tree. And I see
at the park it is pine
tree.

—*Susan Miller*

A Deafula

I went to outside and look at the sky. Everything was blue. I stood up and saw a beautiful apple. I pick up and there are a worm and they bite my finger. I said, "Ow! that hurt a lot." My mother called me "time to take a nap." I told her wake me up at two hours. She said she could wake me up.

I fell asleep fast finally I got dream. It is the same thing happen. When I woke up there are a deafula. And deafula bite my neck. I don't know what I am going to say to my parents. But I am going to keep secret. That is how I got name Deafula. Better watch out for Deafula. But I am the danger one. I need more blood. But I will bit someone. But can't tell Sorry! Now, I can't go outside with lightday, see the lamp with bright thing. But I hate cross. Oh Please don't kill me.

—*Mary Hanks*

I wish Witch and Bats.
The Oz Wizard of Girls and
Lion and Tinman and
Scarecrow.
We Tornado away home
Girl dream bed room.
We will go to surprise.
Girl away walk.
The bats is Black.

—*Anna Turnis*

The Cat
[written about a large, surrealistic drawing of a cat]

There was a cat who makes fires all over the world. The cat has a purple fur with pink stripes. He has red eyes with blue in the center. On his head was a bonfire. He sent fires. He had wings. The color of the wings was red with white spots. The cat had hoofs on it, too.

Whenever he is hungry he usually eat or drink water, ice and snow so it will cool the body for being warm all the time. If he eat or drink fire he will die.

Whenever he is tired he usually go sleep on the moon. If he went to sleep on the sun he will die.

The cat must have the bonfire on his head for one thousand years. It can't get off his head. It's stick to it as tar to it.

It was obey by his mean witch mother.

—*Sallie Jordan*

The star is a yellow.
The door is open.
The face is pale.
I earn money.

—*Kim Bryant*

I looked at sky. It makes me think about snow will coming. I went home. I get my hat & coat & mittens. The outside feels cold. I walked outside.

Later the snow comes. I am happy that snow come. One of snowflakes come to my nose & it melts to water. I wipe off it. Then I am hungry. I need some food. I went home. Then I eat. I looked through window & think about snow. But it stopped. I still looked through window & think about snow. It makes me sad because the snow is stopped. I went to my room & take some nap.

—*Kathy Mingo*

Yesterday was Monday.
Mom was on the table.
I wish make a pumpkin pie.
Mom cook some cakecups.
I don't like angry.

—*Deanna Johnson*

The Ugly Fire

An animal walking down the street. The animal saw a fire on the animal's back. The animal cried. The animal got burn. The ugly fire is gone.

Tomorrow the ugly fire will came back. The animal brought a pail of water. Waited for ugly fire.

Ugly fire came back. The animal throw pail of water. The ugly fire is gone.

—*Mike Bishop*

A boy found a bug and a bug have hurt leg so he take a bug to vet and a doctor fix. Now it is okay. At night the boy take a bug on the shelf so he will sleep all night. The boy wake cuz the bug play with telephone. It bother him. So he take a bug on shelf again. The boy fell to sleep. The bug play a boy's toy. They make lots of noise so the boy threw a rock to the bug so a bug would not bother him again. The boy fell to sleep again until morning the boy remember about a bug. So the boy go to see a bug and the boy take it to vet again. The doctor is sorry for a boy cuz a bug dead!

—*Sheila Robinson*

The animal can eat chair.
The giraffe has number 12 on his body.
The floor can get people and the floor eat all the things.
The floor can run quick then the cars.
The moon can get giraffe and the floor.

—*Crista Wiskus*

Elephant and Fly

The zoo keeper hear elephant scream & scream. So, He walked to the elephant. The elephant is still scream & scream. He wonder what wrong with the elephant. So, He called up to the Vet of Dr. to come & see elephant, then Doctor check up, and He said that the elephant is okay. Later the zoo keeper hear again. So, He went out of the elephant's cage. He talk & talk with the doctor about elephant then the zoo keeper said to the doctor: Hey! Maybe something's wrong with her tail. So, they went to the elephant & the zoo keeper put up the tail. Now they find out the fly is in her ass.

—*Shelly Hambly*

There is no snow at all!
All I see is a bright blue sky!
We harvest food on our table!
When I am trying to think where I started!
And the wind blew my hat away!

—*Anthony Greene*

World War No. II
"About the Supermouse"

The Supermouse can flew over the States. So can do that! I think powerful body, every thing over you. The Supermouse beat me. The Supermouse wonder about the flew away to over the states. The Supermouse can threwn the cannon ball by World War II last day in 1944. I think so The Supermouse isn't dumb? I don't know where is lived in? The Supermouse name is Mighty Mouse.

—*Clint Krogman*

I live home in twin city
am stop on motorcycle
I like to record music
I like to eat potato
I am now fighting.

—*Larry Welch*

All morning, I with my friend going to park. I want walk anywhere. My friend say yes, it is OK. My friend with me walk long. My friend was scared. My friend push me fall sidewalk. I say what matter with you. My friend say, I looked different animals. I never see before. This is cow can fly. I look nothing. You are lie. My friend say I am true to you. No, you just tease me. My friend say look me I nerve my leg. I hate see cow fly. It is bad to you. It is danger to you. I say, you has big fake story. I go to home. I opened door. I was scared come stand on the floor. I am going die.

—*Janice Ludolph*

The land is smooth.
The land is on the water.
The land is under the water and fish and snake and octopus and whale.

—*Danny Froehle*

Zebra

The Zebra always ran on the street.
The Zebra has broken his tail.
The Zebra want eat the sand.
The Zebra magic made the house for his kid.
The Zebra race with turtle.
But the turtle pass the Zebra. The winner is turtle!
The Zebra dig the ground for his baby. The baby was not like the
    Zebra's color.
The Zebra has blue stripe on it!
The Zebra was to free with zoo.
The Zebra want to hurry to get baby out right now.
The Zebra don't have short nose.
            That's all I say.

—*Anita Shepherd*

The Table of Angry

I wish that I could cook a big dinner for the world. But I have one thing that I need that I don't have. It is a table. So I bought one. The table was all set up. I looked at the time. I thought it must be bedtime. So I went to bed. In the morning I looked at the table. It look like an angry bull. The dishes and everything was broken. I got my gun and shot it to pieces and that was the end of the table.

—*Gary Van Surksum*

I dream about boys friend yesterday night.
I saw one girl got big trouble.
My favorite color is blue.
My brother broke his finger before.
I love apple.
I will get dead tomorrow.
I favorite horse animal.
I wish Lou's house is fire.
I did bike on street.

I said ugly other people.
My teacher loves is yellow.
I wish rich of money.

—*Annette McHugh*

The following poem was written about a drawing of an imaginary animal composed of parts of several different animals and other things.

Other people said went to old house. They saw what is animal different. The dog's tail. The lion's face. The moon and star are on the paper. The bug's legs. The house is on the lion's head. The elephant's nose. The bat's wing. The body is bat. The mouse's ear.

—*Mike Miller*

I wish I can drive a car.
I write on a paper.
A rabbit can hop and rabbit have pink ears.
This is printing this is writing.
Clever mean smart.
When I brush my hair I must look at mirror.

—*Lori Sawyer*

I saw a big thunder that start come from the cloud, look at the clock at the store and he was hold a dull yellow book. Wow! I don't believe the thunder could do it.

—*Stacia Barron*

Someone was dream about US Navy.

(war)

We have some trouble with our car.
The car is blue.
I cut my fingernail some day.
The apple is red.

The end of the story.

—*Bruce Butikofer*

THE POETRY CLASS FOR PEOPLE OVER SIXTY

EXCERPTS FROM A JOURNAL

Seventeenth meeting (9/14/75)

Trudy said, "I keep thinking that I'm going to quit coming at the end of each class!"

"Trudy," I asked, "why do you feel that way? I mean, do you really think about quitting?"

"Well, I just don't think I'm a poet. I enjoy coming and listening to the others, but I can't write. Especially during the class meetings!"

"You don't have to. I'm glad enough that you're coming to class."

Which brings up the age-old question in my mind: what is the purpose of the class? My own purpose? Their purpose? The writing portion's own purpose vs. the non-writing portion's purpose? Barry's [Iowa Arts Council program coordinator's] purpose? The Iowa Arts Council's purpose?

The previous immediate answer was: to encourage and teach the people to write poetry. But there is a difference between writing poetry in private and writing poetry in class. Why do the people continue to write in class if they don't want to or don't feel that they can or should? Is it because they like seeing stuff on the Poetry Sheet? Or to please me? Or because they enjoy doing it but are afraid that it isn't "serious"? Or they think it's the "usual" and "normal" way that poetry classes are conducted?

Why do I want them to write? Partly to show them through practice what poetry is all about to me. Partly to encourage them to explore their own ideas at least twice a week. Partly to gather material for the Poetry Sheet and *Speakeasy* [the class magazine]. Partly because the results of in-class writing will mirror the actual success of the class—to a degree (in a way, it's a value system—poetry as currency). Partly because I enjoy seeing how they deal with writing in different circumstances about different things. Partly because it gives a distinct difference to each class—as long as the in-class writing is different each meeting.

A whirlpool of question marks. That's good, though. I hope. It all depends on how easily the "answer-marks" begin to surface.

I found out today that Lee Burton might not come anymore because of an argument with another student over a comma in his poem.

Eighteenth meeting (9/16)

Whew! The class seems to have a real energy of its own—especially noticeable today—a big turnout, twelve, the most so far! I got there at exactly 11:00, and six people were waiting for me. One woman came up to me and said, "I'm leading a relaxation group that meets at 10:30, and I told them that they should continue relaxing by coming to this class."

We went through the Poetry Sheet. There were enough poems on it whose authors weren't present that everyone in class (nine at this point) got a chance to read. Elizabeth C. asked Fanny to read hers. Eliz. H., who came very late, gave me a poem to read for her.

For today's in-class writing, I suggested that everyone write a poem about the fall. I had planned on everyone writing about a day, but we began talking about fall, and the season seemed perfect.

"In order to get into a fall mood, I'll play some tunes on my recorder." I took it out of its case. "I've played the recorder in the College Street park. It blends in very nicely—probably because it's such a mellow instrument."

I took a sheaf of paper, each sheet a different color, and passed it out. "Here's the paper, and now here's the music. I'll play and you can write."

I had decided before class to try this writing because I wanted to play the recorder for them. I didn't really think the idea would carry over into producing much poetry, maybe because it's more abstract than "earliest memory" poems—or "animal poems." More vague. Actually, though, I didn't really want a fantastic response this time. I thought a lull would be okay in the circumstances. Mainly, I'm so busy with so many other things. And the poetry for the Poetry Sheet seems to be increasing.

Anyway, the result *was* fantastic! I haven't had a chance to look again, but I think about nine people—or ten—wrote! All I know is that while I was playing these five songs on the recorder:
"Pass Time with Good Company"
"Ribbon Dance"
"Galopede"
"IrishWasherwoman"
"The Triumph,'
everyone (most) was writing! And with no need for more encouragement or suggestions. The words were flying across the page!

Gulp, I thought, I'm going to have more to type than ever!

Nineteenth meeting (9/18)

We went over the Poetry Sheet as usual, and as usual the readings went very smoothly. The PS provides a vehicle for the class to move within for the first part of the meetings. In other words, it's like a car with automatic steering and power brakes that always seem to work.

*

Alice also turned in a fifty-line poem about NYC! I told her I'd put it on the next Poetry Sheet—but I didn't because I've been so busy working at the post office, studying French, getting stuff ready for the marathon, quitting smoking, etc.

*

Trudy said that her husband, Oscar, didn't like her animal story "Skoda."

"But," she added for the nth time, "you can't really write in class during the last few minutes like that."

"I'm surprised that he didn't like that story. Why didn't he?"

"He thought it was silly."

"Huh! I didn't think so. I liked it."

*

"Next week we're going to have a special in-class writing that I've been thinking about for a while. I'm going to bring a deck of cards so that we can play Poetry Poker!"

"I don't know how to play poker."

"This is a different kind of poker," I replied. "I'll explain the rules next meeting."

Today the in-class writing started at 11:25, since we'd polished off the Poetry Sheet in no time flat. I thought, I wonder how the writing will go by starting this early?

Soon I found out that it was too early. People finished their writing at 10 to 12 and then didn't know what to do—so they began to leave. Thus, there is a good side to beginning the writings late, despite any complaints. It seems that part of the ability to run a class like this involves developing a knowledge of timing.

Gladys turned in her assignment poem, "Professor's Breakfast," and also two poems that her bus driver wrote.

I told them that I'd have to postpone *Speakeasy* till after the marathon on October 9, because I am so busy these days—and also I want to be able to enjoy the fall—what little there might be of it.

Dream (9/23)

I dreamt that there was a poetry contest. The two judges were Alice Gratke and Elizabeth Hajos. They were looking through a pile of poems.

"Is this yours? Is this yours?" they kept saying, as though they were trying to figure out which one was mine.

"No," I said.

They never did figure out which one was mine. Or, if they did, it was after I woke up.

Twentieth meeting (9/23)
POETRY POKER

I got there a little late. I explained that it was partly because I hadn't timed the Poetry Sheet stapling correctly. There were eight pages this time.

After the usual acclimatization with talk about things in general, we began the reading. Again, it went very well.

"Trudy, would you read the group poem for Ann McGeehee? You wrote three of the stanzas."

"Alright."

"Ann had a good cry over this poem," Fanny added.

Anyway, the in-class writing was exceptional this time! We played Poetry Poker. I had typed one phrase on each card in a regular deck a couple of nights earlier. I pulled them out of the paper bag after the group poem was finished.

"Are you ready to play Poetry Poker?" I asked.

They looked very curious. I took out the Dr. Alphabet wooden nickels and passed them around, one per person.

"You could call them the poker chips, but you can keep them instead of betting."

Then I dealt the cards, and the sheets of yellow paper. Each person got five or six cards.

"It's easy to play Poetry Poker. You take the cards and arrange them in front of you, and then use the phrases on them to make a poem. Just try to use all the phrases, but in any order you wish."

"Do we have to use them all?" asked Pearl Minor.

"Well, not really," I said, "but if you don't, you won't have a full house."

After Pearl finished her first poem, she was interested enough in it to ask if she could read it. After she did, I read mine.

Then I said, "Let's trade cards, Pearl. Then we can see how different the results can be even when we use the same phrases."

Voilà! The results were totally cosmic—amazing—wondrous. And what's more, everyone really enjoyed it!

Twenty-second meeting (9/30)

The class arrived at about ten after, and a few minutes later we began reading the Poetry Sheet. The previous classroom writing assignment had been given by Alice Gratke, since I hadn't been there. As I'd suggested, she asked them to write a poem using the letters of their names for the first letter of each line (acrostic poems).

One interesting result of the writing was that some of the people were unselfconsciously egotistic, that is, they wrote about themselves in a very personal I-way that they usually didn't think of doing.

The in-class writing this time: "I've got a list of ten words here. I'll read them for you to take down."

I read them.

"Okay, now we'll write a poem with each line containing one of those words."

"Do we have to use all the words?" asked Velma.

"Not really—no, wait. Yes! You have to!" I said in a mock-serious tone, then laughed. I figured that if they didn't use all, that didn't matter anyway—I'd take their work no matter what, and they knew it. I think they want the direct command not because they don't want to do it that way, but so that everyone will be clear on the ground rules of the poem.

They wrote, and the writings turned out very coherent, despite the disparity of the words.

I reminded them that a week from Thursday I'd be writing the marathon poem around the block. "So next Tuesday I think we'll write a marathon poem in class—to sort of get into the spirit of things. I'll bring some adding machine tape to do the writing on."

Twenty-fourth meeting (10/7)

Began with the Poetry Sheet. Discussed the Poetry Marathon coming up on Thursday. Also reminded them that my mom and sister were coming to class.

For in-class writing, I took adding machine tape out of the bag and said, "I'll be writing the poem around the block as Dr. Alphabet in Poetry City. So why don't we write about Poetry City today? Just imagine what it'd be like with words everywhere. Adjectives, nouns, verbs all over the place."

Twenty-seventh meeting (10/16)

For the in-class writing, I said, "Let's write a poem imagining that we've just met someone from another planet. In other words, you're walking down the street and this person from outer space steps out from an alleyway and asks if you'd like to go for a ride in outer space. How would you reply?"

"That doesn't sound like a good assignment to write out," said Alice G. much to my surprise. "Can't we write about something else?"

Time to pull another trick out of the Alphabet Hat. But I also just learned something: It's a good idea to have an alternative poetry-writing suggestion. Fortunately I'd been thinking of a different writing idea anyway, so I said, "Okay! If you don't like the idea of writing about extraterrestrial visitors, then do this: write a poem using the words *heaven, color*, and *snow* in them, but use at least one of those three words in each line. Thus you'll have a lot of repeats."

"Should we write about the space people and use those words?"

"If you want. Also, you can write both if you happen to feel prolific."

Twenty-eighth meeting (10/21)
POETRY POKER 2

Today the reporter from the *Daily Iowan* came to class to do an article. I'd met her at a party over the weekend after the Grand Opening of the Puppet House by the Eulenspiegel Puppeteers. Somehow we'd gotten to talking about the class, and she said she'd like to do an article on it, so I suggested that we meet today at Hamburg Inn #1 at 10:30.

"I was trying to figure out what in-class writing to do today. From what you said at the party, I figure I ought to have them write about a specific kind of memory, but I finally decided to do a more experimental type thing. Today we'll play Poetry Poker, because out of all the assignments thus far, that was the one everyone seemed to enjoy just about best."

"Uh, I'd prefer that you did one using their memories, rather than giving them the words. I think that I'd rather see how all those thoughts they've had through their lives would make them feel about things."

"Oh, OK. We can do something else. But anyway, here's the Poetry Sheet with the first Poetry Poker writing on it. It was a lot of fun and had amazing results."

She read some of them. "Wow, these are great. Do the Poetry Poker thing. You know more about them than I do."

Joan is twenty-eight, married, a former journalism student who has begun working for the *Daily Iowan*. She's very likeable and easy to talk to. She got along well with the class. She sat between Alice Gratke and Pearl Minor. They talked to her the most. When the article finally came out, they formed the bulk of it.

"Today we'll play Poetry Poker again. As we did earlier, I'll deal out this special deck with each card containing a different phrase. Just use the phrases in any order, adding your own words in between."

I dealt as Dom (a *Daily Iowan* photographer) snapped photographs. Joan joined in on the writing. After people finished they read theirs and Joan read hers, too.

The Poetry Poker results were great.

"Next time," said Alice, "we should get new cards. I keep seeing the same phrases."

Twenty-ninth meeting (10/23)

At the multilith place, Sandy Johns, the woman who takes my order and also helps me choose the colors for the Poetry Sheet (since I'm color-blind), suggested that I leave the last page of Poetry Sheet #26 blank (and white).

"Why? It sounds like an interesting idea, but. . . ."

"Well, we make the first seven pages all fall colors, then the eighth page is white for snow. Then you ask them to write about the white blank page and why it's there. See if anybody can guess the reason."

It was a great idea. So I did it.

*

THE WHITE PAGE

We read the Poetry Sheet through, then I asked them to write on the white page about what the white page symbolized. I explained that the woman at the copy center had a specific symbolism in mind, but that they should write what they want. So they wrote. I said that I'd write the answer, since I knew it.

All but Elizabeth Countryman wrote about the page in its relation to the act of writing. Elizabeth wrote about fall.

I told them to watch for the article, and that it'd be in the *Daily Iowan* Friday or next Monday. I also mentioned that I talked to Larry Eckholt of the *Des Moines Register*, and that he might come next Tuesday to do an article.

In the following days (before the next meeting) I decided that I'd like to do a very special writing for Larry's visit. It turned out that Joan's article, entitled "Poker: Poet's New Method," attracted a lot of interest *because* of the Poetry Poker idea. And I was a little concerned that the idea might turn people off.

Anyway, to make it short, I decided to build a Poetry Castle. More about that when the time comes.

Thirtieth meeting (10/28)

I carried the Poetry Castle over, as well as the new Poetry Sheets, Elmer's glue, and Dom's photos of the class and the Poetry Marathon.

We read the Poetry Sheet, which included The White Page writing from last time, also two pages of new works by class people, also the "Poem around the Block," which we read by each of us reading about eight lines. When Julia Kondora finished reading the last line of the Marathon poem, Alice said to me, "Now you read what's left, Dave."

"Dr. Alphabet."

Alice smiled.

The writing this time was supposed to be the Poetry Castle, but since the reporter didn't show up, I suggested a Halloween Poem.

"We'll write some Halloween poems by using a list of ten words specifically chosen for the mood. Like the last time we used a list, this time you should try to use one or even two words per line. If you don't want to use any in a line, that's okay, too. But no more than two."

Everyone wrote the ten words as I read them, and everyone wrote a poem. Julia Kondora, usually prolific, had difficulty with the poem, so I helped her.

People began reading their results. Great!

"These should be printed as a little Halloween book for children," said Alice.

Thirty-first meeting (10/30)
POETRY CASTLE

Larry Eckholt of the *Register* came to class today. He interviewed Alice, Fanny, and Nellie. Alice and Fanny's replies were very nice and positive, but Nellie's responses were amazing!

Larry: "How long have you been taking the class?"

Nellie: "I've been in it for only a few weeks now. I started a little later than the others."

Larry: "Why are you taking the class?"

Nellie: "I'm taking the class because it gives me an outlet for my feelings. I get to be with people, and that helps me now. During the past six months I've had some very bad times. My sister died six months ago, and I was there with her. Then my mother died a couple months after that. And my husband died eight months ago. So I've had some very difficult and lonely hours trying to deal with such things. It's been very hard. And I realized that one of my main problems was that I didn't have any friends. I was so lonely that I dwelled on my own problems instead of going out and seeing people. Then I heard about this poetry class, and I thought I'd see what it was like."

Larry: "Do you like it?"

Nellie: "Oh yes, this class has helped me so much. I have friends in the other people here, and poetry gives me an outlet for my inner feelings. I wouldn't be able to do so otherwise. I hope the class can continue."

She was very intense and emotional in what she was saying. It seemed that she was on the verge of tears. I sat there with my mouth open in surprise. I'd never realized her situation. Larry took an occasional note. All in all, we were both amazed. She continued to elaborate on her feelings and situation a little while longer, then she was silent. She'd said enough.

*

It began at 11:40. I took the brown plastic bag off it, and placed it in the center of the table. I scattered the magazine cut-out words around it, on the blue railroad board that I'd set the Castle on (where the blue overlapped from the bottom of the Castle).

"In honor of Halloween, we're going to create a Poetry Castle. Everyone says that poets build castles in the air. Well, we're going to build one right here on the table!"

We began glueing the words down. I asked Larry Eckholt to join in, and he did. This event went great! I took some photos. At noon, no one wanted to leave for lunch. Steve Schneider, the meals coordinator, started telling them to come eat.

"The poets will have to join us now!" He was at the other end of the Gloria Dei auditorium where the lunches were being served. The people continued to glue their poetry. Finally he came over and asked again.

"Hey, you people. It's time for lunch. You can't live on poetry."

"Not unless you eat your words!" said Julia.

They went to lunch. I stayed to answer further questions from Larry. After lunch, three people came back to continue with the Castle. One of those three was Steve! We continued for another hour. (Larry left at about 12:15.)

Thirty-second meeting (11/4)
POETRY MOBILE

We went over the Poetry Sheet as usual. This time they were somewhat surprised at the results. I had typed up the poetry fragments from the Castle.

"I can't make any sense out of these," said Louis.

"Well if you could," said Trudy, "then it wouldn't be poetry."

I have to admit that the results were the most fragmented thus far. But still I thought there was some great stuff. So I tried explaining my point of view.

"Just look at some of these little fragments as being slogans, or tiny epigrams, etc. For example: FREE THIS BOOK or HOW NOW, GURUS."

They could see that that made some sense. But when I handed out the in-class writing, Trudy said, "Do you want them to make as little sense as the Poetry Castle fragments on this sheet?"

"I'd prefer more sense than in those," I said.

This led into the in-class writing, which was the Poetry Mobile.

"I'd like to give each of you one of these Poetry Mobiles that I made."

The mobiles were each made out of three irregular differently colored pieces of posterboard attached by fishing line. When the top end of the fishing line was held, the mobile hung down with each segment one above the other, free to spin.

"The City Library is going to display these mobiles."

They wrote. The results were crisp little autumn imagist poems (mostly). This was surprising, since even the haiku page in one of the earlier Poetry Sheets had failed to get that response.

Ten people wrote (one was me). The results are now hanging in the City Library between eight brick columns.

Thirty-third meeting (11/6)

The last meeting for this four-month funding period. At this point, I feel we can begin going in directions that are new to everyone. The Poetry Castle, Poetry Poker, and Poetry Mobiles were a breakthrough for my own ideas about writing and teaching. I've got a notebook with thirty new ideas that combine poetry with the plastic arts. Soon to come: The Technicolor Page, Mirror Writing, Foam Rubber Poems, Alphabet Roulette, etc.

"Now that we know the class will continue for another two and a half months, I'd like to tell how it'll be structured. I've been thinking a lot about where to go from here. Since we meet two times a week, I think we'll divide the meetings equally so that on one day we'll do Memory Poems and on the other day Imagination Poems. With the Memory Poems, we'll delve into previous experiences in order to recapture them in poetry. The writing method will be rather traditional, pencil on white pages. The Imagination Poems, though, will be written using experimental techniques, like the Poetry Mobiles."

Before the in-class writing, I asked Fanny to read from Whitman's "Song of Myself," and then his "Spider." I then suggested that everyone read some Yeats for next week. Then I read "Sailing to Byzantium." The response to this poem was fantastic. When I read the last lines— "Consume my heart away; sick with desire / And fastened to a dying animal / It knows not what it is; and gather me / Into the artifice of eternity"—Gladys Edwards looked astonished and said, "Oh, God! God!" It really struck a chord in her!

When I first mentioned Yeats's name, Fanny said that she remembered he was the one that Joan Titone in the *Daily Iowan* compared her to.

It has worked! The class went great for four months! End of first session. . . .

Thirty-fourth meeting (11/11)
TECHNICOLOR PAGE

There were three women from Des Moines sitting in on the class to observe for the Iowa Arts Council. They picked a good day to do it. First, the Poetry Sheet was interesting. Second, the in-class writing would be very different. Third, at the last minute I remembered to shave. Thus, we were all ready.

*

"Today we'll begin this new ten-week session by going from the white page to The Technicolor Page." With that I took the specially prepared pages out of the box and held them up one at a time, asking "Who'd like this one?" till everyone had one. I gave one to each of the observers, too. They didn't really want to join in, though, so two of them returned the pages, while one kept hers and said she'd write a poem on it and send it. We'll see.

The writing started. Some of the people wrote directly on the page, but most wrote on a white 8 1/2 x 11" first, then copied it! Each chose a specific way to fit the shapes.

I'd told them to write about the rainbow: "Imagine that you're walking down a street through a woods, and you find pieces of a broken rainbow laying on the ground. You pick them up and put them on a single sheet of paper. Then you write about why the rainbow was broken.

"For instance, a rich man decides to have a stained-glass rainbow erected in the fall, since there are no rainbows in winter. The neighborhood kids are playing baseball, and they accidentally knock the ball into the rich man's rainbow. The rainbow shatters into a thousand pieces and crashes to the ground.

"You can each make up your own story to explain why it's there. Or you can write about what the broken rainbow symbolizes."

The observers said they enjoyed the class. The people were also excited about the article that appeared in Sunday's *Des Moines Register* about the Poetry Class.

"When I went to church Sunday, three or four people came up to me and said they saw my picture in the paper," said Nellie. "I didn't know what they were talking about until someone showed me the article."

"Someone said to me, 'Gladys, I saw your picture in the paper,' and I said, 'Oh my, what for now?'"

Pearl said, "I really liked your poem 'On Poetry City,' Alice. That's one of the best ones I've seen written in class."

Thirty-sixth meeting (11/18)
FOAM RUBBER MOON

I had to make two trips from my place to the Methodist Church to carry over the ten pieces of foam rubber that I got from the Physics Building yesterday.

Myldred (jokingly): "If I don't get a Poetry Sheet, I won't come anymore." I'd forgotten to give her one.

"Does anyone have any paper that we could use for today's writing?"

Fanny passed out sheets from her tablet.

"This is the first part of the writing. First, I'd like you to write down five things that you associate with the moon."

We wrote.

"Now we'll write five things that are associated with the earth."
And wrote.

"Okay," I said, getting up from the table and walking across the room to the partition behind which I'd hidden the chunks of foam rubber before most of the people arrived.

"Let's pretend we're on the moon. We look up at the earth. It looks like a blue sphere."

"A blue jewel," said Pearl. "The astronauts described it as a blue jewel."

"Yeah. A blue jewel spinning through space. Each of us is alone on the moon. We have nothing to write on, but we do have a magic marker and a laser device. Using the laser, we cut a chunk out of the moon to write on. And here are the moon-chunks. . . ."

I brought the foam rubber over to the table. It was a sort of faded yellow foam rubber. Each chunk was a rectangular 3D shape, about 18" x 6" x 6".

"This is what we'll write on—and this is what we'll write with— magic markers."

I emptied out a bag of ten magic markers on the table. They each took one. The writing began—confusedly at first.

"I don't think I'm going to write today," said Louis. "You've gone too far this time. I think I'm going to just walk around."

Louis had given me the Technicolor Page that he'd taken home with him and said he'd write on.

The writing was a h-u-g-e (in every sense of the word) success. Everyone seemed to really enjoy it.

"I was talking to a friend of mine, Dave," said Pearl, "and I told him about your class. He said that you'd make a good kindergarten or primary teacher. The things you have us do are things that would really go over with kids."

"Yeah, but all ages should be able to enjoy any good teaching methods."

"Well," said Pearl, "we should all be children at heart."

"Right!" added Fanny.

"You know," said Pearl, "we are like kindergarten kids the way we want to show Teacher our work right after we've written it: 'Here! How do you like mine?'"

Trudy and Gladys each took a chunk home with them to finish and bring back on Thursday.

Steve Schneider [the previous site manager] showed up and joined in on the writing.

Forty-third meeting (12/16)
POETRY PUPPETS

The Eulenspiegel Puppet Theater came—Terri, Monica, and Jenean. They each had a puppet, and they wore rouge and gold makeup, as well as their performance costumes.

We read the Poetry Sheet—while the puppets and puppeteers sat and listened (and the puppets occasionally commented on the poems).

"Last Saturday night I did a little poetry performance with Duck's Breath Mystery Theater. It included a rewritten version of 'Frosty the Snowman,' called 'Frosty the Poet.' Since this is the season for caroling and all, why don't we sing it? Everyone knows the tune." ("Frosty the Poet" was reprinted on the last page of the day's Poetry Sheet.)

I wasn't sure how it would work. Suddenly, though, everyone was singing. Fanny Blair was the one who got the ball rolling. It was wonderful. I only regret that I didn't tape it, but I didn't even think about doing it till just before it happened.

*

"Now the puppets and the puppeteers are going to do a little show."

They did a three-way skit for about fifteen minutes, then broke while Monica left the room. During the break, they and the puppets talked to the people. And the people talked back, as though the puppets were real people. Louis Taber and Nellie Voelckers seemed to get the biggest charge out of it all—though everyone was very involved.

Monica returned in a special troll outfit, and she told a story to the class. Louis laughed aloud a number of times (as did the others, only Louis set the record). . . .

Forty-ninth meeting (1/20/76)
POETRY PAINTING

Poetry Painting, the in-class writing, was a gigantic success, ranking alongside Poetry Poker and the Poetry Castle.

"I brought these little canvas boards and some paint. Each of us can take one of these felt-tip pens and dip the one end in the paint and paint an abstract painting on half of the canvas, then write about what you see in the colors on the other half. Here's the paint."

I squeezed some blobs of red, blue, green, and yellow onto the round aluminum paint-tray and passed it around for everyone to dip their pens in. They made paintings, then wrote haiku-like short poems. (It's amazing how different exercises result in different-length poems.) The results were beautiful combinations of words and colors, both playing off each other.

Some of the people remarked that they couldn't paint in class like that, *but*—the interesting thing is that despite what they said about it, they still dug into the paint with a passion—and once the paintings were done, writing the poems seemed simple. No one said they couldn't write poems in class (though they don't always say that anyway).

Louis Taber, however, declined to write. He paid me $1 instead.

(At lunch with the class:) "Be sure to come Tuesday, a week from today. We'll be doing the biggest in-class writing yet—the Poetry Robot."

Fifty-first meeting 1/22
POETRY ROBOT (PREVIEW)

Whew! It took a huge amount of work, materials, and energy to build the Poetry Robot. I carried it in two trips over to the Methodist Church. The only one there was Fanny.

"I'll bet you got some looks on the way over."

"Oh, yeah. I think I'll hide the Robot behind the partition here. I've got to go back home for the arms."

*

". . . And here is the Poetry Robot." I pulled the curtain back, and there he stood, seven feet tall, with five colors of posterboard and silver trim twinkling at the edges. The face had features made out of wooden letters. The eyes were a green *A* and a blue *B*, the nose an apricot *X*, and the mouth two red *Y*'s laid with tops touching.

"I can't write on that," said Louis. "I wrote a description of it, though."

Which reminds me, before opening the curtain and revealing the Robot, I gave them a preliminary assignment.

"To get into the right mood, why don't each of you write a description of what you think the robot will look like. How tall? What colors? What are its eyes, nose, and mouth made of?"

"Should this be a poem?" Pearl asked.

"Not especially. Just a description. Consider it a pre-poem."

As it turned out, everyone did write in poem-form, so when anyone wants to know if they're supposed to be writing a poem, the answer is yes. At least at this point. (It used to be the other way around. That's progress!)

After writing, each person read the pre-poem that he or she wrote. They were really interesting.

*

". . . And here is the Poetry Robot."

"What's his name?" asked Gladys.

"The Cardboard Bard."

"Bard? Oh, that means poet," said Louis.

Everyone but Louis and Barry [the Iowa Arts Council program coordinator who'd come to observe] began glueing the words that I'd cut from magazines to make sentences on the Robot. While they glued, I took about twenty photos. Then I glued, too. I regretted having to miss part of the glueing by photo-taking instead. I was beginning to really enjoy doing it when lunch time began.

Bill, the janitor, said I could leave the Robot there at the church, and Fanny said she'd pick up the words—and we'd continue Thursday.

Fifty-second meeting (1/29)
POETRY ROBOT

The Poetry Sheet this time contained the "guesses" as to what the Poetry Robot looked like. We read the poems, discussed the new ones (a poem by Fanny, a poem by Myldred).

Edna Gingerich dropped by. "I just came in to get a copy of the Poetry Sheet," as she has done many times.

"Why don't you stay and work on the Poetry Robot?" I asked.

"Because I don't think I can learn anything from it! And that's the main reason why I either come to class or don't come to class."

"Okay. But you could just do it to enjoy it."

"I think it's ridiculous!"

At this point, I was at a loss for words, so I asked the wrong question: "Why do you think it's ridiculous?" (Actually, I could've guessed her answer, knowing what she's said in the past. The question wasn't really wrong though, since it led into a very good discussion about the value of the "multimedia" or prop-type writing.)

"Because it's the thing you'd expect grade school kids to do!"

We'd discussed that aspect of the writings at other times. However, the Poetry Robot was, in a sense, an ultimate writing. I was disturbed by Edna's comment, but later I realized how valuable it was—and how honest.

"I don't mean to sound off like this," she continued, "but I want to do things that will help me increase my knowledge of poetry. This doesn't do it."

"I can appreciate your honesty, Edna, but I didn't build this without realizing that some people could interpret it that way." I didn't really know how to validly or clearly explain why I built the Robot, other than to say I thought it would be an enjoyable writing, as it seemed to be.

Edna left to help get ready for the congregate meal. She was collecting the money. I had to face the class, and I figured that we should definitely discuss Edna's point of view. If for no other reason, because I wanted to know for myself:

1) Why I built the Robot.

2) Whether it was a valid and worthwhile project for a class of people sixty and older. Feeling somewhat defensive, I said to the group:

"I hope everyone here realizes that I didn't intend for this Robot to be a joke. I meant it as a serious and enjoyable—somewhat different—writing. I wanted everyone here to feel good about working with it."

"Oh, gosh," said Fanny. "As you go through life, you'll meet plenty of people who won't like what you're doing. You'll just have to accept that and continue on."

"I've already met a lot of people like that."

"I enjoyed working on the Robot. It's a fantastic creature," said Benita. "And I don't feel funny about it. Picasso said, 'It takes a long time to grow young.'"

"Yeah, that's it!" I replied. "And I'll bet Picasso would've liked the Poetry Robot."

"I'm sure he would've," she said.

We talked about it a while longer, then I got out the glue bottles and the words, and we started on the Robot once again.

ALTERNATIVE POETRY WRITING METHODS CLASS

AUDIOTAPE TRANSCRIPT

Recently I have been teaching a summer staff development course called Alternative Poetry Writing Methods: A Whole Language Approach for elementary and secondary school teachers. The course runs for a total of fifteen hours over three days, with each day divided into two sessions of two and a half hours each.

Each of the six sessions has a main topic: 1) Introduction to Classroom Poetry Writing Methods; 2) Physical Poetry; 3) Environmental Poetry; 4) Wordplay and Game Poetry; 5) Puzzle and Permutational Poetry; and 6) Roundtable Discussion. In addition, the students (teachers) write poems using some of these methods.

In the roundtable discussion of the most recent course, the students and I brainstormed ideas for using these methods and for inventing others. The students' approach to poetry was enthusiastic, imaginative, and energetic, and their sense of humor kept the discussion lively. I taped the last hour of it. The students were Robin Alvarez, Vito Bellardinelli, Jan Blankenberg, Becky Collins, Brenda Danker, Chris Dutson, Charlene Engstrom, Myrna Folker, Sharon Pilling, Judy Slobodnik, and Elissa Swafford.

DAVE: The Word Calculator and the Poetry Kaleidoscope in particular—how would you use them?

CHAR: With the kaleidoscope, if you had the child take a poem that they've already written and cut it up into little pieces, they could stick their pieces in and just turn it and see what they come up with—if the poem still means the same or if it's real different from the original.

ELISSA: I like the idea of coming up with a word, like your name or something, and seeing if there are words that relate to that one word, then copying those down and using those words to write. I think it's a fun way of coming up with different vocabulary.

SHARON: I tried five words but could only get one real word so it might help with gibberish too.

BRENDA: I think a non-poetry use of the Word Calculator would be in spelling where students manipulate the circles to spell out their words.

This would be good for students who have learning disabilities. Those students would like it because it's fun, too.

BECKY: You gave us several different ways to come up with word lists, phrases, maybe one-liners, to write poetry from. I think that fits into it possibly just as well, a little bit more fun and time-consuming. It's another way of finding words and putting them down and manipulating the words to form poetry.

MYRNA: You could use it with rhyming words. You'll get that on the last strips and twirl the other ones and come up with the list of ten rhyming words, what you were talking about this morning.

DAVE: How would you get the rhyming words?

MYRNA: Well, you'd get your ending sound on the last three—*ain* or whatever you want, *ake*—and then. . .

JUDY: . . . see what happens.

MYRNA: Then you'll use the beginning letter or blend of letters.

DAVE: Oh, you mean to search for rhyme, like I have *fine*, and then I can just turn this and come up with *dine*.

MYRNA: Or you might want to turn two strips, or three sometimes.

JUDY: Oh, that's a nice idea.

MYRNA: And children will like to do that. I'd find that very usable with children.

BECKY: And they might be able to come up with maybe not actual true dictionary words that rhyme with one another, but they can make up words. A lot of times, depending on the beginning sound, it may sound close enough to another word that they could substitute it and give it their own meaning within the poem. It's a forced rhyme, just for fun, silliness—

MYRNA: —like Dr. Seuss.

BECKY: Yeah, like Dr. Seuss-type stuff. Start out with a real word and then make up your own rhyming words just spinning those first few letters and saying it and seeing what does this sound like, 'cause kids do that. They'll pick up on the sounds of words and just repeat them ad nauseum. So that would be good for that too. I like that idea, finding rhymes with that.

JUDY: Anything that gets them away from that blank piece of paper. I call it "blank-paper-itis." If they have something in their hands they can work with, they're away from that blank piece of paper. They don't have to look at it, and they'll come up with something that'll fit. And work.

JAN: You could use a larger drum [to make the Word Calculator]. Instead of one letter in a square, have words in a square. On each strip there might be some blanks so that as you put one phrase then on the next strip you might have a blank to show a space.

BECKY: When you hit those blanks, somewhere along the line you might be able to fill in your own words or phrases to personalize it, instead of sticking only with whatever you can come up with. As you turn the rings of words, you could manipulate it to get the spaces where you wanted, and then you could reword phrases.

JAN: I think I'd have some blanks in each strip, so if you came up with "THE RAN something," if it didn't make sense, then you could fix it and leave it or change it or whatever—add what you want.

JUDY: It would be a way of making this moveable.

BECKY: To attach them around the drum, use Velcro, and then they can change the placement of the strips, which would make your possibilities endless with a few word strips. Put them on and off. If you're going across the curriculum you can choose vocabulary which goes with the science unit, and they can write—come up with sentences or phrases that have to do with whatever they're studying, including vocabulary words, which they would have to use correctly in a sentence or a phrase.

ELISSA: It's a good teaching tool because we know that the more different ways and media that we use to try to teach, the child is more likely to recall and remember. This would be another fun way of presenting the vocabulary.

BECKY: And another thing—maybe pull this into a reading activity—your word strips could include names of people and places and things in a particular story, and they see if they can line words up to say something about the character from that story.

JAN: Or even a poem.

BECKY: That's right.

JAN: Then you'd have these words, and see if they could line up phrases from the poem or ideas from the poem.

BECKY: If we put Velcro on it, they can move the strips to make it work for them.

DAVE: Then you'd have two ways of moving. Not only rotating, but actually ripping off.

BECKY: And moving it to a different position.

MYRNA: That has endless possibilities for kids.

DAVE: What about these glasses? ["Writing Glasses," made by rubbing six letters of transfer type randomly on each lens of a regular pair of eyeglasses.]

MYRNA: The letters need to be smaller.

JAN: Maybe little words instead of the letters.

JUDY: You could use them as poem-writing or storytelling glasses. You've seen the continuous stories where you go down the line and one person says a line and the next person says another line. You could use them as a prop for that kind of thing, if they could get past the giggles. I mean, those are really funny to look at.

DAVE: They could be a general prop for somebody who goes in and does storytelling for kids. You tell them you're going to read a poem to them, and the poem is on your glasses.

JUDY: I think you've created a character there.

MYRNA: Or maybe you could play a game, "What Do I See?" This'd be a fast-moving game where all the group would use it, but the first one puts them on and turns around and says, "What do you see?" and you have to say the word, and he puts them on and says "What do you see?" and the next one has to say the word he sees, and so on.

JAN: And then you could introduce a new character called "Little Red Reading Hood."

DAVE: Then Little Red Reading Hood could get together with Little Red Writing Hood.

GROUP: Wooo! (*laughter*)

DAVE: Shifting the subject a little, somebody else was mentioning the idea of the Poetry Shirt and—

ELISSA: —using the shirt as a gift. For a classroom project, that they're actually going to give this shirt to someone, a student teacher or a retiring teacher or an administrator. And so their poems would have to be geared toward either that person or their position, like "A teacher is" or about a principal—and it'd have to be positive things. That would be a great gift.

JAN: Reminds me again of my apron that I talked about this morning, the gift from the neighborhood. They put "Best wishes, we will miss you" and then their names. That gift means a lot to me, and it's a wonderful remembrance. I can see how the Poetry Shirt would be a really nice gift.

ELISSA: The kids would really have to work hard to make a decent poem. It'd have to be something where they took some time, knowing that it was going to be forever with this person, and really incorporate their skills.

DAVE: The senior citizens wrote theirs separately on a piece of paper, and then revised them. In doing something like that, you're not writing directly on the object, but you're creating with the object in mind. Also the student is revising, too, and that's important.

BECKY: It would be neat if you knew ahead of time that you were going to be writing something for a T-shirt, and then could form your lines so that they're in the shape of a T or in the shape of a T-shirt. It would appear like a T-shirt on the T-shirt, which would be even more of a challenge.

JAN: A T-poem.

ELISSA: Another idea as far as clothing goes, hats would be a good one, the different hats that we wear—"mother," "teacher," "wife." The students could make different hats for a person, like, you know, your principal is also a father. They could write what they think a father is, and that would be another gift, a collection of hats.

DAVE: Were there any of the writing methods that seemed particularly suitable to any particular age group, or that either would work better than others, or any that might not work well?

JAN: Just about any of them can be adapted. I don't know why not. I mean, you could go from one simple letter to a phrase to a paragraph depending on the age. You can do a lot.

DAVE: But what about this [Letter Galaxy board]? It would have to have a basement age, wouldn't it? For instance, could you do it with first or second graders?

JAN: The way you could do it with them, you could do math and reading and all that together and ask, "How many *b*'s can you find?" They'd have to count all the *b*'s. But it would have to be bigger.

JUDY: Even first graders could find some words.

JAN: You could draw a line through it. How many in the top? How many in the bottom? There'd be some spatial concepts. How many right and how many left, how many up, down, words like that that they need to become familiar with when they're little.

JUDY: I was even thinking of using it for ESL students and the lower reading adults I'd be working with, just finding words that they know.

BECKY: Also, if you enlarged it and there was more space between the letters for younger kids, you could manipulate by adding your own letters or maybe whiting out other letters so that the vocabulary they're familiar with would be more obvious to them. If you wanted to work with it, you could spiral up or down.

DAVE: What about the uses of the puzzle activities or the game activities, especially when all of the words have been provided, not just a few? Like the Haiku Maze. What value would that have?

ROBIN: Haiku Maze would attract the students that were reluctant to get into it or "I can't write poetry." They can't have an excuse then 'cause the words are right there in front of them.

BECKY: If you're doing a unit or something that's going to carry on over a period of time, these types of things would be the good icebreakers. Like she said, just to kind of play around with poetry and not be responsible for producing on your own. You're just kind of playin' around and seeing what happens. Then little by little they do the types of things where they fill in their own words in blanks to make two versions of the same poem or something before you actually say, "OK, here's that blank piece of paper. Now go for it."

If they've had a lot of time playing around and seeing how things turn out, they might be a little bit more relaxed about it. Which is what I think I will probably use some of these things for—just brief little introductory things before we actually study the types of poetry and read examples of different kinds. No way do I want to stand up there and say, "Okay-y-y-y, guys, today we're starting the Poetry Project." You know, it's—

UNIDENTIFIED PERSON: Agggggghhhhhhhh!

BECKY: Yeah, exactly.

ELISSA: This Dollar Bill Limerick—it'd be fun to start off just putting four columns on the board and saying, "Okay," and going around the room, "give me unusual adjectives." And as they list them out, write them in column 1. Et cetera. Then when it's completed, they've made their own words for each column. Then hand out the Dollar Bill Limerick with the blanks and say, "Okay, we're going to use the words you made. Fill in the blanks here." It would show them how different it sounds when you use more unique or specific words than just—

UNIDENTIFIED PERSON: "Good."

ELISSA: Yeah, lower vocabulary words. The feeling's much different, the picture's much sharper, and so they can see there's a difference in it.

ROBIN: That'll teach them parts of speech too. You ask for adjectives, and the smart ones will immediately blurt out something that'll get the other ones, "Oh, that kind of." So that'll give *them* a chance.

ELISSA: I really find that junior high students are so limited in being able to come up with vivid and exact words to meet what they feel, and they need lots of exercises. This really stretches their imagination and their vocabulary so they can believe that they can actually come up with something that sounds pretty neat.

DAVE: Do you think that the methods that we talked about would have different uses or applications in general; for instance, writing poems on objects compared to writing in an environment compared to wordplay poetry or game poetry or puzzle poetry? A specific example: how would writing a poem on a piece of paper taped around the school affect students compared to writing a poem with animal names in it?

JAN: When you're writing around the school, you probably think, "Well, if I mess up, nobody's going to notice 'cause there'll be so much that it won't show up as wrong or not as good as someone else's."

ROBIN: Those are different ways of expressing, too. Around the school, that'd be graffiti-like, and they could deface the building: "This is my way to get at the building." Then the animal names and vocabulary and definitions and—

BECKY: Well, writing about animal names is primarily a test of thinking skills. Most kids are not taught purposefully to write anything standing up. Writing outside, you'd probably be using markers or big chalk. Plus, it's going to be paper on probably brick, and if it's the older brick it's probably going to be that real rough-type stuff. So it's going to be a physical activity as well as coming up with the words to write down.

DAVE: The students can write poems individually, or they can collaborate in different ways. How do you think that difference would affect them?

ROBIN: Some students excel in little small groups, and others excel in doing it themselves.

JAN: Maybe they should be given a choice: "Do you want to work alone or with a partner?" Some would rather have all the credit, and some wouldn't want anybody to know that they have anything to do with it.

BECKY: Since we're talking about writing poetry here, I think we can assume that this is going to be done a number of different times. You don't do poetry in a forty-five-minute block one day during the school year. It's something that happens, so give them the opportunity to do both. Just have it directed. "Today I'm going to pair you off" or "I'm going to put you in groups of three." And other times say, "This time you're going to do it by yourself." Some kids are going to produce better in the different settings, but they've had a chance to do both. You get to see what happens when they do both, as a group and individually.

ELISSA: There'll always be kids in the group that will let the leaders take over. They'll always let someone else do the work if they're willing to. And there's always kids that are willing to do most of the work.

I think that what I've gotten from this course—and I would like to have my kids experience it, too—is that they can all be confident that they at some level can express their thoughts and ideas, and that each student should come to that point where they're confident enough that, "Hey, I can express something and it can be poetry." They're only going to get to that point if they do things on their own at some point. All of these ideas help that, and all these different games and exercises are great.

JAN: Also, when it comes to grading—if that's what we have to do—or evaluating, just always remembering that there's no wrong poetry, that a child's expression is his expression, that "What you write is good, because you wrote it. It's you."

CHRIS DUTSON: So when you are evaluating children's poetry, you should always write something at least positive, and maybe that would keep all the people from saying, ten, fifteen, twenty, or thirty years later, "I'm scared to death of poetry." If they experience some positive comments from the teacher when they're young. . . .

DAVE: How about thinking for just a minute about some way you could write poetry in an unusual way. [*Pause.*] Who wants to go first?

BECKY: I guess I'll go first. What I was thinking of was having some kind of paper that either is a certain color and when water touches it, it changes color, like a litmus paper type "dealy," or it wrinkles severely like seersucker or something, so that they can write with water. Or— they're for little-bitty kids—they call them Paint-with-Water. It looks like a plain old sheet of a coloring book, but when they color over it with water, color will appear in the different spaces. You might even have a big huge sheet that has a rainbow of that. Then when they paint with the brush, so they spill water, big deal, you don't have to worry about any mess. Their letters come out rainbows. I still like the wrinkled one. If I could find a paper that would really shrivel so that you'd have this buckley-type thing where the words are all written in wrinkles. Boy, I oughta quit teaching and develop that and patent it and away we go!

ROBIN: As far as painting with water, just have them write their poem in water on a sidewalk, and it would disappear. And that would give them a thing in the classroom: "How did it feel writing your poem and then it disappeared? How'd you feel putting your words down and then they're gone?"

With the wrinkled paper, an art project would be to wrinkle up paper, smooth it out, and look at the lines. Sometimes you see people's faces in it. And then write something about that. I was also thinking that a subway train or a train, writing a line or a phrase on each car. Then they switch the cars.

JAN: How about "Eating My Words"? You could make finger jello, and cut it into tiny cubes, and then the children could cut phrases or words or a teeny little poem out of the finger jello, and then eat it!

DAVE: Sounds delicious.

MYRNA: I was thinking along the same line. I guess we like to eat. This is outlandish, though. I probably wouldn't ever do it. But why not have a taffy pull, and as you're pulling the taffy, make the letters for the poem, and then you end up eating it.

DAVE: Just have a whole feast. Everything is made with letters.

VITO: The custodians would blow up your room.

JAN: "The Poetry Palate."

CHRIS: One method I used ever since I was young, I like the beats that are in songs. If I was in the mood to write poetry, all I had to do was go put a Diana Ross album on. There's something about her music that'll get me writing poetry in a minute, and whatever I'm feeling, it'll just come out. But it'll come to the beat of her song, so actually what I'm doing is probably plagiarizing or something. No, really, I'm taking the beat of her music and adding my own words.

You can do that. You could take songs and just make up symbols together. OK, when we hear this, one beat, it's going to be this symbol. Have the symbols on the board, and then replace the symbols with words, and that way you're studying beat and pattern and syllables.

Another thing I've wanted to do with kids is to listen to a song from a historical period—it could be the sixties, it could be the Civil War—but a song from a historical time. Figure out the beat. You talk about what are they trying to say, what are they feeling, and then show that there's a connection with history, that our feelings were no different twenty, forty years ago than they are today.

Let's say this song is about sending someone off to war. Well, we just did that with the Gulf War. Then let's brainstorm all kinds of words that the Gulf War reminds us of and replace that beat with all the words we had brainstormed until we created another song. So actually you're writing your own song from your own history. But you have to do that with older kids.

JUDY: I pictured a small school with lots of sidewalks, and children would go out with little rocks to make the words, the letters, and put a poem clear down the sidewalk.

DAVE: How do you mean using the rocks?

JUDY: To make the letters. Laying them.

BECKY: Or colored beans, so it would show up a little bit more. It's probably easier to just find a whole big bunch of rocks and let 'em go at it. But if you want something that's more striking to the eye, you could use—

JAN: —all those math manipulators.

BECKY: Yeah, all those math manipulators that sit in people's closets. Start dragging some of that stuff out.

ROBIN: If you want to stay with food, you could use M & M's, and when everything was finished, they could copy it and eat their M & M's.

DAVE: How about spelling out a poem on the sidewalk with birdseed, and then seeing how long it would—

MYRNA: Yeah. I think it should be something from nature. Outside.

BECKY: Well, you probably need to develop some type of applicator.

JAN: Peanut butter!

BECKY: That'd be a mess. For the birdseed, I mean, some type of real small something to kind of funnel it through so that they can guide it rather than trying to sprinkle it.

TWO VOICES IN UNISON: Write in the peanut butter first, and then just sprinkle it.

JAN: Talk about an irate custodian!

ELISSA: It'd be fun to put in the peanut butter "Feed the Birds" and then put the seeds, and then there it is.

BECKY: You could put it on something. You could get a board or something and then leave it out rather than leaving it on the sidewalk. You *never* want to antagonize the custodian. That's the one person you must always be nice to.

JUDY: Speaking of birds, I thought of trees. There are some Asian cultures that write things on paper strips and then tie them to trees like prayers or wishes for the coming year. That could be rain-forest wishes or endangered species wishes.

DAVE: People used to write or rubber stamp political statements on dollar bills and spend them. One could write poems on dollar bills or have a rubber stamp made of a short poem of yours and just stamp all the money you have till the FBI—

JUDY: —knocked on your door. It's totally illegal.

DAVE: No, it's legal.

JUDY: Oh, is it? I've been told it's not.

DAVE: As long as you're not destroying them.

CHRIS: You don't deface the dollar. Just put a few words on it.

DAVE: Yeah, you're helping it. Anybody else have any methods?

JUDY: I've kind of gotten off on the idea of writing on things ever since you said the Poetry Chair. That never entered my mind. Pieces of clothing like your belt. Around the belt. I was thinking on the lines of a gift for a man. A suitcase would be good.

CHRIS: A tie.

JUDY: There's all kinds of things, now that you think of it, that you can write on.

BECKY: I just thought of another way. Take a piece of dark construction paper, black preferably, and write the poem on it. Then take a safety pin or a straight pin or maybe something a little larger and poke through all the way along your letters. When you put it up to a window or a light, your poem would shine through.

POEM WRAPPING A CITY BLOCK
PERSON-IN-THE-STREET INTERVIEWS

How do people really feel about a poem that becomes a part of the environment? On October 9, 1977, as I and others wrote the Poem Wrapping a City Block, Paul Ingram taped 167 interviews with people as they passed by the wall of words.

People of all ages participated by suggesting words and ideas and by writing their own poems on the paper. It was not a school-sponsored function, but many children came by to see "the guy in the hat" writing poetry on the walls. This poetry marathon was the prototype for several poems wrapping schools.

Paul's interviews captured the spirit of the day. In the excerpts below, which express both positive and negative reactions, Q is Paul, and A is the person interviewed. The number after each A places the answerer in sequence. A5 means the fifth person interviewed.

Q: Would you mind telling us how it feels to be in Poetry City, sir?
A6: Warm.
Q: Good. Good. How about you?
A7: A B C. Thank you.

*

Q: How does it feel to you, sir, being in Poetry City and watching this poem being written?
A12: I think it has the makings of a revolution, and it puts fear in my heart.

*

Q: What do you think of the public poem, ma'am?
A16: I should've brought my pom-poms.

*

Q: How does it feel to be constructing Poetry City?
A19: Oooh. It's very nice. Very good feeling inside. You know, it's all of us little people in the back that really make it work, you know.

*

Q: I think he's improvising.
A29: He's improvising?
Q: Yeah. Just needs to get flowing. Just needs to get flowing. What?
A30: He should have lunch first.

Q: If you had a favorite word—like if you had to utter one word for the rest of your life—what would it be? Maybe he'll put it in for you. Well, take your time. Think.

A40: Oh, wow: *maybe.*

Q: Thank you, sir.

A41: *Love. Love.*

Q: Good. What's that word?

A42: *Strawberry.*

Q: *Strawberry*! How about you, sir?

A43: Uh. *Jock.*

A45: I'm impressed by the way he has the word *turn* written here right on the corner.

Q: He's turning the corner.

A45: I think he's combining the language with the sculptural aspects.

A44: What? Is this the media is the message, or what?

A45: No, the turn is the corner. That's all.

A44: The turn is the corner?

A45: You don't want to over-generalize here.

*

A46: I think poetry—public poetry—is a real gas. I think people should do this all the time. It would sort of lose its novelty, but still it would be fun.

Q: Would you like to do it yourself sometime?

A46: I think I could probably muster up the audacity to do it maybe.

Q: Thank you. Would you like to write one of these yourself, ma'am?

A44: Yes, indeed!

*

A48: I think it's crummy!

*

A54: I think it's pretty good, but I think he's crossing out a lot of things maybe to make a little more space to make sure he makes it all the way around the block.

Q: Would you care to respond to that, Dr. A?

Dr. Alphabet: She's absolutely right.

*

Q: If you could utter one word for the rest of your life, and only that one word, what word would you choose, sir?

A57: *Word.*

Q: Thank you. Can you work that in sometime, Dr. A?

*

Q: A comment on Poetry City, sir?

A67: G-gosh! Um. It's highly superior to most towns that I've wandered through.

*

A75: I think it's a good idea. I think it's good for exposing people to different kinds of literature and new ideas and stuff.

Q: Thank you, thank you. How about you, ma'am?

A76: It should be condemned, and all poets put in jail.

*

A82: I think it's pretty stupid.

Q: Thank you, sir.

A82: I still think it's pretty stupid.

Q: Thank you again, sir.

A82: They wasted all this paper. They could start feeding all the poor people in New York.

Q: Could I get some real people? What do you think of this, sir?

*

Q: What do you think of Dr. Alphabet's Poetry City Marathon?
A105: I don't know what to think of it. I don't know what to make of it. What is all this? "Elvis Presley"? What's this "Elvis Presley"? "The onions"? "Waves"?
Q: Well, you'll have to ask Dr. A himself about that.
A105: That's Dr. A over there?
Q: None other.
A105: Wow! Who does his laundry, or his tailoring?
Q: Hand-made.
A105: Hand-made?
Q: He does it himself. Yeah.
A105: Far out. Great. Wonderful.

*

Q: What do you think of this whole thing, ma'am?
A120: Oh, I think this is the most wonderful thing I've ever seen in my entire life.
Q: Really?
A120: I just can't believe it.
Q: Oh, that's great.
A120: Yes. I'm saved.
Q: Fantastic, but I'm biased. Say that again.
A121: Reminds me of the old Iowa City.

*

A131: I like the idea. I saw him kick it off, and I knew if he kept writing that big that he wasn't going to—he'd get around the block in far less than six hours.
Q: Well, it's—he's halfway through time-wise, and he's much less—he's about a quarter around the block.
A131: Oh, well, I think I'll follow him on around.

*

Q: What do you think of Dr. Alphabet, kids?
A133: I like him.
Q: You do? Okay.
A133: Yeah.
Q: Do you like him, too?
A133: He's neat-o.
Q: What do you think?
A134: I like him, too.
A135: He's nice.
A136: I like him.
A137: Uh, he's funny.

Q: What do you think of the idea of writing poetry in public?

A145: Oh, I don't know. It's just—it brings everybody together. I think it's—whether you call it poetry or writing or whatever, you know—it's just kind of nice to see everybody down here.

A149: It's far out. It only happens once in a while.

Q: I know.

A149: It's great when it does.

A150: Thank God.

A155: It's quite an extravaganza.

Q: Why do you think someone would do such a thing?

A155: Why, for the same reason that one would frolic in a field of daisies.

Annotated Bibliography

This bibliography includes several different kinds of books. Some of them may not seem to deal directly with literature, but all of them are full of good ideas that can be adapted for a poetry writing class. They are imaginative, well written, and enjoyable. (I have immodestly included two books of my own.)

Books

Aarons, Trudy, and Koelsch, Francine. *101 Language Arts Activities: Games, Gameboards, and Learning Centers for Early Childhood Education and Special Needs Children.* Tucson, Ariz.: Communication Skill Builders, 1979. Original games for learning letters, words, and sentences. Many of the games could be adapted for poetry activities.

Amis, Kingsley, ed. *The New Oxford Book of English Light Verse.* New York: Oxford University Press, 1978. A large collection of humorous, satiric, and witty poems by well-known and lesser-known poets.

Benét, William Rose, ed. *The Reader's Encyclopedia.* New York: Thomas Y. Crowell, 1965. A staff of 34 experts assembled thousands of entries on all aspects of world literature: authors, titles, characters, literary movements, forms, terms, awards, etc.

Bergerson, Howard W. *Palindromes and Anagrams.* New York: Dover, 1973. In this wide-ranging study, Bergerson gives a brief history of the two age-old forms and presents a generous selection of the best lines and poems containing them.

Borgmann, Dmitri. *Language on Vacation.* New York: Scribner's, 1965. The first book treating wordplay as a field of knowledge to be studied in its own right. Well organized and full of examples.

Brown, Rosellen, et al. *The Whole Word Catalogue 1.* New York: Teachers & Writers Collaborative, 1972. Divided into assignments and materials sections, this book describes a myriad of intriguing ways to write poetry, based on classroom experiences.

Byrne, Josefa Heifetz. *Mrs. Byrne's Dictionary of Unusual, Obscure, and Preposterous Words.* Secaucus, N.J.: Citadel, 1976. The author lists and defines words that she considers the most outlandish examples from other dictionaries.

Calas, Nicolas, and Calas, Elena. *Icons & Images of the Sixties*. New York: Dutton, 1971. A survey of the predominant artistic trends of the 1960s, including Pop Art, Lettrism, Assemblage, New Realism, and other movements.

Collom, Jack. *Moving Windows: Evaluating the Poetry Children Write*. New York: Teachers & Writers Collaborative, 1985. A thorough discussion of how to evaluate children's poetry, as distinct from that of adults. Collom discusses the aesthetics in the 300 or so example poems written by his students.

Commire, Anne,, et al. *Something about the Author: Facts and Pictures about Authors and Illustrators of Books for Young People*. Detroit: Gale Research, 1971–present. This long-running series of reference books presents information on many children's authors and illustrators, excerpts from book reviews, photographs, illustrations, and even addresses and phone numbers.

Coody, Betty. *Using Literature with Young Children*. Dubuque, Ia.: William C. Brown, 1992. For use with children ages one to eight, this book has two purposes: to present some of the best children's literature for the age range indicated, and to offer methods for using it with children.

Dow, Marilyn Schoeman. *Young Authors Conference: Kids Writing for Kids*. Seattle, Wash.: The Write Stuff, 1985. This practical work minutely describes how to organize a young writers conference. One chapter gives "idea makers" based on word lists, fill-in-the-blanks sentences, and similar pencil-and-paper writing methods.

Eastman, Arthur M., ed. *The Norton Anthology of Poetry, Shorter Edition*. New York: Norton, 1970. Perhaps the most widely used anthology in undergraduate English programs, this book presents English and American poetry from the 13th through the 20th century. Includes many helpful footnotes.

Edgar, Christopher, and Padgett, Ron, eds. *Educating the Imagination: Essays & Ideas for Teachers & Writers*. 2 vols. New York: Teachers & Writers Collaborative, 1994. A wide-ranging collection of essays on ways to explore poetry writing, playwriting, and other forms. A selection of the best articles from *Teachers & Writers* magazine, this book offers many ideas for anyone interested in the creative use of language.

Ellmann, Richard, ed. *The New Oxford Book of American Verse.* New York: Oxford University Press, 1979. Poems from the 17th century to the present. A companion volume to the Helen Gardner volume below.

Firpos, Patrick; Alexander, Lester; Katayanagi, Claudia; and Ditlea, Steve. *Copyart: The First Complete Guide to the Copy Machine.* New York: Richard Marek Publishers, 1978. According to the authors, photocopying can be an art. Many examples from "copyartists" back up the authors' contention.

Gardner, Helen, ed. *The New Oxford Book of English Verse.* New York: Oxford University Press, 1979. A widely respected anthology of English poetry from 1250 to 1950. A companion to the Ellmann volume above.

Gardner, Martin, ed. *The Annotated Night before Christmas.* New York: Summit Books, 1991. Dozens of parodies of this Christmas classic demonstrate how a poem can inspire imaginative spinoffs. The original text and 91 variations are included, with introductions and footnotes.

Geller, Linda Gibson. *Wordplay and Language Learning for Children.* Urbana, Il.: National Council of Teachers of English, 1985. Geller analyzes the spoken wordplay of children: riddles, puns, nonsense words, and parody. Student examples from the playground and the classroom accompany the discussion.

Harmon, William, ed. *The New Oxford Book of American Light Verse.* New York: Oxford University Press, 1979. This gathering shows the distinctive flavor of American humor.

Hansen-Krening, Nancy. *Competency and Creativity in Language Arts: A Multiethnic Focus.* Reading, Mass.: Addison-Wesley, 1979. Approaching language from several different points of view, including poetry, art, creative drama, and nonverbal communication, the author shows how multiethnic materials can be used to teach basic language arts skills.

Hart, James D., ed. *The Oxford Companion to American Literature.* New York: Oxford University Press, 1978. This volume provides ready references to authors, writings, and related topics. It also includes more than a thousand summaries of important American novels, stories, essays, memoirs, poems, and plays.

Harvey, Sir Paul, ed. *The Oxford Companion to English Literature.* New York: Oxford University Press, 1974. The first part of this volume presents a listing of English authors, literary works, and literary societies; the second part explains common literary allusions.

Hemphill, Herbert W., Jr., and Weissman, Julia. *Twentieth-Century American Folk Art and Artists*. New York: Dutton, 1974. This well-illustrated book presents the work of 145 untrained artists, whose works display the same freedom as that of children's art.

Hendrickson, Robert. *The Literary Life & Other Curiosities*. New York: Penguin, 1981. In this intriguing compendium of odd facts about writing from ancient times to the present, Hendrickson revels in the Ripley's-Believe-It-or-Not side of literature.

Horn, Maurice. *The World Encyclopedia of Cartoons*. New York: Chelsea House, 1980. A huge reference work covering all aspects of cartooning. The more than 900 cartoons make it entertaining, too.

Johnson, Paul. *A Book of One's Own: Developing Literacy through Making Books*. Portsmouth, N.H.: Heinemann, 1990. This manual describes 23 different traditional and non-traditional formats for making books.

Koch, Kenneth. *Rose, Where Did You Get That Red?* New York: Vintage, 1974. A double-edged technique for involving children in the enjoyment of great poems of the past and present by having them write poems inspired by the greats.

Kohl, Herbert. *A Book of Puzzlements: Play and Invention with Language*. New York: Schocken, 1981. Kohl presents familiar and unfamiliar wordplay forms, and describes how students can use them.

Kostelanetz, Richard, ed. *Dictionary of the Avant-Gardes*. Pennington, N.J.: A Cappella, 1993. This reference guide to various forms of avant-garde art, music, and literature shows many different approaches to creative work.

Lederer, Richard. *Crazy English: The Ultimate Joy Ride through Our Language*. New York: Pocket Books, 1990. Humorous essays that reflect the idiosyncracies of the English language, including odd plurals, animal names, and palindromes. The book's accessibility has brought it a wide audience.

Lehman, David, ed. *Ecstatic Occasions, Expedient Forms: 65 Leading Contemporary Poets Select and Comment on Their Poems*. New York: Macmillan, 1987. Each poet provides a poem and an essay about the internal and external events surrounding the poem's creation.

Lloyd, Sam. *Sam Lloyd's Cyclopedia of 5,000 Puzzles, Tricks & Conundrums with Answers*. New York: Pinnacle Books, 1976. This classic 19th-century collection by an American puzzle genius is full of picture riddles, word games, mathematical problems, and other "species of mental gymnastics."

Mapes, Lola. *Name Games: Personalized Language Games and Activities*. Nashville, Tenn.: Incentive Publications, 1983. Mapes shows many creative ways to use names of all sorts as motivators for language learning: writing poetry, making up wordplay, drawing pictures, creating crossword puzzles, etc.

Melton, David. *Written & Illustrated by . . . : A Revolutionary Two-Brain Approach for Teaching Students How to Write and Illustrate Amazing Books*. Kansas City, Mo.: Landmark Editions, 1985. Melton feels that every child can and should make a picture book. He shows all the steps, from inspiration to publication, for making a book in the traditional rectangular format.

Miller, Joni K. and Thompson, Lowry. *The Rubber Stamp Album: The Complete Guide to Making Everything Prettier, Weirder, and Funnier: How and Where to Buy over 5,000 Rubber Stamps, and How to Use Them*. New York: Workman, 1978. Miller and Thompson trace the history of rubber stamp art and provide many current examples of rubber stamp art.

Morice, Dave. *How to Make Poetry Comics*. New York: Teachers & Writers Collaborative, 1983. A step-by-step guide for combining poetry and comic strips in the classroom.

Morice, Dave. *Poetry Comics: A Cartooniverse of Poems*. New York: Simon & Schuster, 1982. Poetry by 34 poets adapted to cartoon form, including Shakespeare, Donne, Herrick, Blake, Shelley, Tennyson, Whitman, Dickinson, William Carlos Williams, and Ginsberg.

Newby, Peter. *Pears Word Games: Over 150 New and Traditional Games for All the Family*. London: Pelham Books, 1990. This collection of spoken and written games demonstrates the versatility of words, which serve as game pieces as well as linguistic symbols. It includes classics and contemporary games.

Padgett, Ron. *The Teachers & Writers Handbook of Poetic Forms*. New York: Teachers & Writers Collaborative, 1987. This handbook defines

74 forms and genres, gives historical information, quotes examples, and, unlike similar manuals, suggests ways to use the forms in class.

Preminger, Alex, ed. *The Princeton Encyclopedia of Poetry and Poetics*. Princeton, N.J.: Princeton University Press, 1974. Updated periodically, this renowned reference book goes into great detail in discussing world poetry. With articles by 215 scholars, it is the most comprehensive book of its kind. Also exists in a condensed version.

Queneau, Raymond. *Exercises in Style*. Translated by Barbara Wright. New York: New Directions, 1981. Queneau tells an unremarkable story of a man accusing another man of jostling him on the bus, and then he retells it in 99 different established and invented ways.

Rothenberg, Jerome. *Revolution of the Word: A New Gathering of American Avant-Garde Poetry 1914–1945*. New York: The Seabury Press, 1974. This anthology draws together nontraditional poems by well-known and lesser-known 20th-century figures. Includes biographical notes.

Sears, Peter. *Secret Writing*. New York: Teachers & Writers Collaborative, 1986. A step-by-step approach to language through a discussion of codes. The book starts with a game of Hangman, explores topics such as invisible writing, nonsense, tap dancing, difficult literature, and hieroglyphics, and ends with the Arecibo space message.

Tiedt, Sidney W., and Tiedt, Iris M. *Language Arts Activities for the Classroom*. Boston: Allyn and Bacon, 1978. A large collection of poetry and prose writing exercises, word puzzles, speech games, and many other ways for students to explore language.

Williams, Emmett, ed. *An Anthology of Concrete Poetry*. New York: Something Else Press, 1967. A global look at sound, shape, and other kinds of concrete poetry in its formative years, 1945–1967. Many works in English and other languages appear with notes and translations.

Zavatsky, Bill, ed. *One-Line Poems*. A special issue of *Roy Rogers* magazine, winter, 1974. The only anthology of one-line poems ever published.

Ziegler, Alan. *The Writing Workshop*. 2 vols. New York: Teachers & Writers Collaborative, 1981 and 1984. Ziegler discusses the classroom as a writing workshop, with advice on how to write and revise as well as how to deal with touchy subjects such as plagiarism. The book contains many imaginative writing exercises.

Magazines

Games. Available at newsstands and in supermarkets, this bimonthly magazine includes crossword puzzles, cryptograms, and other word games, from simple to complex. Six issues: $17.97. Address: Games, One Games Place, P.O. Box 55481, Boulder, Colo. 80322-5481.

Word Ways: The Journal of Recreational Linguistics. The only magazine devoted to all aspects of written wordplay, from humorous essays to serious studies, from puns to poetry to computers and beyond. Four issues: $17. Address: Word Ways, Spring Valley Road, Morristown, N.J. 07960.

Dave Morice

The Teachers & Writers Handbook of Poetic Forms, edited by Ron Padgett. This T&W bestseller includes 74 entries on traditional and modern poetic forms by 19 poet-teachers. "A treasure"—*Kliatt*. "The definitions not only inform, they often provoke and inspire. A small wonder!"—*Poetry Project*. "An entertaining reference work"—*Teaching English in the Two-Year College*. "A solid beginning reference source"—*Choice*. "You can't get a quicker, smarter course"—*Millenium Whole Earth Catalog*.

Poetry Everywhere: Teaching Poetry Writing in School and in the Community by Jack Collom & Sheryl Noethe. This big and "tremendously valuable resource work for teachers" (*Kliatt*) at all levels contains 60 writing exercises, extensive commentary, and 450 example poems, all "presented with clarity and common sense" (*The Independent*).

Educating the Imagination, Vols. 1 & 2, edited by Christopher Edgar & Ron Padgett. A huge collection of 72 informal essays with ideas for teaching poetry writing; fiction writing; playwriting; writing about folklore, history, and science; translation; writing across cultures; bookmaking; writing parodies; creative reading; and much more.

Personal Fiction Writing by Meredith Sue Willis. A complete and practical guide for teachers of writing from elementary through college level. Contains more than 340 writing ideas. "A terrific resource for the classroom teacher as well as the novice writer"—*Harvard Educational Review*.

Playmaking: Children Writing and Performing Their Own Plays by Daniel Judah Sklar. A step-by-step account of teaching children to write, direct, and perform their own plays. Winner of the American Alliance for Theatre & Education's Distinguished Book Award. "Fascinating"—*Kliatt*.

The Story in History: Writing Your Way into the American Experience by Margot Fortunato Galt. Combines imaginative writing and American history. "One of the best idea books for teachers I have ever read"—*Kliatt*.

The List Poem: A Guide to Teaching & Writing Catalog Verse by Larry Fagin defines list poetry, traces its history, gives advice on teaching it, offers specific writing ideas, and presents more than 200 examples by children and adults. An *Instructor* Poetry Pick. "Outstanding"—*Kliatt*.

The Writing Workshop, Vols. 1 & 2 by Alan Ziegler. A perfect combination of theory, practice, and specific assignments. "Invaluable to the writing teacher"—*Contemporary Education*. "Indispensable"—*Herbert R. Kohl*.

The Whole Word Catalogue, Vols. 1 & 2. T&W's bestselling guides to teaching imaginative writing. "*WWC 1* is probably the best practical guide for teachers who really want to stimulate their students to write"—*Learning*. "*WWC 2* is excellent. . . . It makes available approaches to the teaching of writing not found in other programs"—*Language Arts*.

❖

For a complete free catalogue of T&W books, magazines, audiotapes, videotapes, and computer writing games, contact
Teachers & Writers Collaborative
5 Union Square West, New York, NY 10003-3306, (212) 691-6590.